Maynooth College is two hundred years old. Age is honourable and achievement is to be honoured, and both age and achievement will be widely celebrated on the bicentenary. The occasion will see the celebration of Maynooth's original purpose, still continued, the training of priests for Ireland. It will also mark the development of that purpose over two centuries, eventually to include third-level education of men and women in philosophy and theology, in the sciences, and in the arts.

To honour in an appropriate way these two hundred years of teaching, members of the college staff are publishing a series of books in a number of academic disciplines. Edited by members of the College Faculty, these books will range from texts based on standard theology courses to interdisciplinary studies with a theological or religious involvement.

The venture is undertaken with pride in the long Maynooth academic tradition and in modest continuance of it.

GREEK PHILOSOPHY
AND THE CHRISTIAN NOTION OF GOD

Gerard Watson

Greek Philosophy and the Christian Notion of God

the columba press

First published in 1996 by

the columba press

93 The Rise, Mount Merrion, Blackrock, Co Dublin

Cover by Bill Bolger
Origination by The Columba Press
Printed in Ireland by
Colour Books, Dublin

ISBN 1 85607 112 X

Contents

Preface

In his preface to *The Theology of the Early Greek Philosophers* (Oxford 1947), Jaeger said that 'In a second volume, against the Pre Socratic background, I should like to treat the period from Socrates and Plato down to the time when, under the influence of this tradition of Greek philosophical theology, the Jewish Christian religion transformed itself into a theological system in the Greek manner, in order to force its admission to the Hellenistic world (p.v.).' The second volume was never written, unfortunately. Even for Jaeger it would have been a large task, and yet it seems that a volume of this sort is worth attempting.

What follows here does not claim to be the book that Jaeger would have written. It is an attempt to show how the Greek tradition of natural theology became part of the foundations of Christian theology. The restriction to natural theology means that specifically Christian doctrines like those of the Trinity, Incarnation, Redemption and Predestination will be left out.[1] The Semitic contribution to the formation of Christian theology is, for the most part, ignored here because there already exists a large body of specialised and general studies in the area. The Greek tradition has not been analysed to the same extent in general studies, partly because it falls between various disciplines and partly because it is frequently held that the most influential system of Christian theology, that of St Thomas Aquinas, is pure Aristotelianism served in Christian vessels and no more needs to be said about it. Specialist studies do not share the last error, but the very fact that they are specialist has meant that their findings are not yet widely known among students of the philosophy of religion. This is regrettable for a number of reasons.

Firstly, in the last thirty years, there has been a great deal of study of the relations between Plato and Aristotle and possible mutual influence, study largely stimulated by the work of Jaeger himself earlier in the century.[2] The arguments for and against a developing gap between Plato and Aristotle continue, and the arguments about when the disagreement began. In that discussion questions connected with the theology of Aristotle have occupied an important position. But his theology has hardly been considered in its own right and there has been a certain reluctance to see theology as an important element in Aristotle's mature thought. We shall have to try to see if that reluctance is justified. There has not been the same reluctance with regard to Plato's theology, but in the English-speaking world (for which this book is primarily intended) one reading the literature on Plato might be justified in thinking that theology was a relatively unimportant part of his thought. This was not the way in which his followers in Middle and Neoplatonism read him for many centuries after his death, as I hope will be clear from this book. These were the Platonists whom the Christians knew and used when they were formulating their own theology and, as a consequence, the Platonists were of very great importance for Christian theology.

Secondly, and arising from what I have just said, in recent years there has been a welcome increase in the volume and quality of work published in English on later Greek philosophy and a fruitful linking of studies in philosophy and patrology. But these areas are so vast that the non-specialist is intimidated by the bulk of the introductory reading required in order to gain some familiarity with the questions, and is appalled at the obscurity of even some of the names of the philosophers, not to mention the highly scholastic issues which are occasionally debated. Partly as a result of that, and partly as a result of the Greekless state of even some trained philosophers and theologians nowadays, there is a danger that the theological speculations of the Greek philosophers may be consigned to the dustbin where Aristotle's cosmology went long ago. This would not only result in an undesirable gap in their knowledge: it would also give rise to a distortion in the whole understanding of Christian theology.

I shall concentrate on the theology of the pagan philosophers down to the time when the philosophers themselves became Christian, and when in so doing frequently became theologians primarily and philosophers only in a subsidiary capacity. I wish to show how Greek philosophy passed into Christian theology and therefore I consider a man like Marius Victorinus, for example, who exemplifies the change from the old to the new world in his own life and thought. Marius stood between the Greek and Latin world, making Greek Neoplatonic speculation available in Latin. But generally I shall ignore the Greek Fathers of the Church whose influence was not directly felt in the Latin Western world, even though they were themselves influenced by Greek philosophy and even when they were men as great as Clement and Origen. The main channels, however, for the passage of Greek pagan thought into the Christian Latin world of the West were Augustine, Boethius and the Pseudo-Dionysius, and I shall consider them from this point of view. These men illustrate how congenial Platonism was to Christianity, and will be considered simply as philosophers who happened to be Christians and who, through their philosophy, helped to give Christian theology what might be called its classic shape in the works of Thomas Aquinas.

Even with these restrictions, the field is still very wide, and contains many questions much disputed among scholars. I shall often have to be content with indicating further reading where the issues are discussed in more detail. I shall end with a glance at the thought of St Thomas as an indication of how Greek thought had been assimilated in a comprehensive expression of Christian faith by a man who was a Christian theologian but also a great philosopher.

I wish to commence this study with Plato, but for the sake of continuity with Jaeger's book I begin with a brief sketch of the background to Plato, where I do not give much more than a list of important influences. I refer readers to Jaeger for a proper discussion of the matter. Then I shall turn to Plato and his pupils and successors. Any book of this sort which tries to deal with Plato in a relatively short space faces an initial difficulty, the danger of falsifying Plato by confining him to a fixed system. As Wallis says in another context: 'Plotinus' aversion to formal systems is equally due to the conviction he shares with Plato that Reality evades expression in rigid formulae'.[3] Plato deliberately avoided the construction of a neat closed system so that he might stimulate people to think for themselves. We have to impose some system on his thought in order to discuss it at all, but it is important to remember that Plato is deliberately flexible. I shall therefore try to indicate the approaches to theology which he favours in his work, and the passages from his writings which were most cited by later Platonists. Plato is, I think, the most important Greek influence on Christian theology. This belief may seem to be belied by the relative shortness of my chapter on him, but in a sense the whole book is about him, and he is easily available in good English translations. If the voluminous literature about him were considered for its possible relevance to his theology, the book would never get beyond Plato. The same applies to others, an outstanding example being Augustine. He as the most important Platonist for the Christian Latin world, and in his case I have given somewhat more space than usual to biographical details which explain how this came about. In general there is a tendency to incline towards brevity rather than length, but it seems better to provide a guide to a number of important thinkers in manageable compass than to try to analyse them all in exhausting and off-putting detail. The book should be accompanied by the reading of the excellent specialist studies I refer to and upon which my dependence is obvious.

CHAPTER ONE

The Presocratics And Socrates

Xenophanes is the first of the Presocratics whom I wish to consider for his possible influence on Plato, and I single him out because it might be easy to overlook him. Aristotle speaks with no great respect of Xenophanes in his resume of the views of his Presocratic predecessors in the first book of his *Metaphysics*. But he does state that he was the first man to insist that all that is remains a unity, and goes on to report, rather hesitantly, that he is said to have been the teacher of Parmenides. (*Met.* 986b21-27) Since we are concerned here with inherited notions, whatever their source, which Plato in particular passed on, and since there is no doubt that Parmenides was a supremely important influence on the latter with his arguments concerning the unchanging One, we need not delay further in trying to estimate the exact contribution of Xenophanes to the creation of this enduring concept. Nor are we concerned primarily with his statement that the One is the god. The idea of his which does interest us, and which does seem to have made a big impression on Plato, and thereby marked all later philosophical theology, is his declaration that God is unlike human beings.

Xenophanes says this in various fragments and it is difficult to believe that Plato had not Xenophanes in mind when in the *Republic* (378Cff) he criticises the way in which the poets have presented the gods. Xenophanes says that the entertainment at dinner should start with hymns, and warns 'Give us no fights with Titans, no nor Giants nor Centaurs, which our fathers falsely told.' (Fr. 1. Guthrie trs.) Like Plato, he is particularly critical of Homer, largely because he was of such importance in Greek education. (Fr.10) 'Homer and Hesiod have attributed to the gods everything that is a shame and reproach among men, stealing and committing adultery and deceiving each other.'(Fr. II. Kirk and Raven trs.) Not only should we not demean the gods by telling such stories about them: we should be wary of thinking of them in human terms at all. 'Men think that the gods are born, and that they have clothes and a voice and a body like their own.' (Fr. 14) They shape them in their own image: 'The Ethiopians say that the gods have snub-noses and are black, while the Thracians give them blue eyes and ginger hair.' (Fr. 16) The logical conclusion would be that 'if cattle and horses or lions had hands, ... horses would have gods shaped like horses and lions like lions, and would make them have bodies like the bodies they have themselves.' (Fr. 15) But God is utterly different: 'There is only one God, greatest among gods and men, similar in no way to mortals, either in body or in thought.' (Fr. 23) God is what Aristotle would call the Unmoved Mover, and his activity is described in terms of which both Plato and Aristotle would approve: 'He always remains in the same place, not moving at all. It is not fitting for him to go here and there at different times, but without any labour he makes all things shake by the thought of his mind.' (Fr. 26 and 25)

These statements are striking, and it seems likely that they influenced Plato and Aristotle also, in spite of his strictures on Xenophanes. The last two fragments quoted will take on a different form in Parmenides to whom we shall shortly turn. I have repeated the other fragments from Xenophanes because they are fundamental to the movement in Greek theology against anthropomorphism, and because they are less accessible than the passages in Plato which they inspired, or indeed most of the tradition of 'purified' theology which they helped to mould. But to Plato the thinking of Parmenides appeared to be more radical concerning God, and Parmenides' influence has, through Plato and then more particularly through Aristotle, lasted to this day, while the more primitive attitudes which Xenophanes was attacking no longer need the same attention. Plato must, however, have found Xenophanes sympathetic in many ways. The famous fragment 34 will have appealed to Plato's well-developed consciousness of man's limitations: 'No man has seen the clear truth about the gods, nor will there ever be a man who knows about them and all the things of which I speak: for even if he should happen to speak the full truth, he himself does not know it; mere opinion is worked into all things.' This gives no more grounds for complete scepticism than the gloomier utterances of Plato himself, and Plato would have fully approved of fragment 18: 'The gods did not reveal all things to mortals from the beginning, it is by searching that, with time, men find out all things better'.

In spite of that, Aristotle, as we have indicated, did not single out Xenophanes as an important influence on Plato. He begins chapter six of Book One of the *Metaphysics* by saying: 'After the systems we have named came the philosophy of Plato, which in most respects followed these thinkers, but had peculiarities that distinguished it from the philosophy of the Italians.' (Ross trs.) He has just been talking about the Pythagoreans, and just before that Parmenides has been mentioned. Aristotle explains the peculiarities by pointing to the effects of the Heracliteans and Socrates on Plato. We may now glance briefly at these people in turn.

We begin with the Pythagoreans. The difficulty of distinguishing Pythagoras from the Pythagoreans is notorious, and it was felt from a very early stage. We cannot be sure of the form in which Plato knew the philosophy, even though, as Guthrie says, it is the Pythagoreanism which Plato knew which we would especially like to be acquainted with.[1] But we know this at least: Plato evidently admired, for the sake of moral education, the Pythagorean linking of astronomy and harmony. (*Rep.* 530) Salvation would come through 'philosophy'.

Part of the reason for Plato's interest in, and admiration for, mathematics is the relative certainty which they provided because they were concerned with unchanging truths. His appreciation of mathematical certainty would have been increased through his contact with Heracliteanism, at least in the form in which Aristotle summarises the Heraclitean doctrines: 'that all sensible things are ever in a state of flux and there is no knowledge about them.' (*Met.* 987a33f) Most people would agree that Plato retained that tenet of Heracliteanism 'even in later years'. But this was not the only part of the teaching of Heraclitus which made a deep impression on Plato. He mocked the Heracliteans for 'plucking from their quiver little oracular aphorisms to let fly at you' (*Theaet.* 180a. Cornford trs.) but these were the *epigoni*, not the master himself, and Plato must have enjoyed Heraclitus' own unrelenting use of paradox to drive home the truth about the unseen realities. The man who wrote in the symposium (192D): 'The soul of each lover is clearly longing for some mysterious thing. It cannot find words for this mysterious experience: what it longs for is wrapped in riddles, obscure as oracles' must have admired someone who felt the need of modeling himself on the god of Delphi, who neither speaks out clearly, nor yet hides his meaning, but gives a pointer to it through a sign. (Heraclitus Fr. 93) Heraclitus' deliberate use of ambiguity to provoke questioning was followed by Plato's use of the dialogue to interrupt dogmatic slumbers. But Plato liked not only Heraclitus' style: he also accepted wholeheartedly Heraclitus' strictures on the senses. 'Eyes and ears are bad witnesses to men when they have souls that do not under-

stand their language.' (Fr. 107) Men's worthless certainties are attacked by Heraclitus in terms that are not significantly different
from those later used by Plato. 'Compared with God, the wisest of
men seems like an ape in wisdom, beauty, and everything else.'
(Fr. 83) 'Human nature does not judge truly, but the divine nature
does.' (Fr. 78) Heraclitus was evidently prepared to ridicule
anthropomorphism as bitingly as Xenophanes had done. And
finally, however far in the end Plato may have moved from his
earliest theory of Forms, he would always have welcomed Heraclitus' conception of a *Logos* which was at once the unseen plan of
things and a God of many names who ruled the universe and harmonised all the apparent discordancies in it. Here at least Heraclitus would have combined with Pythagoras to sustain Plato's belief that the universe was formed on a systematic pattern.

Yet in spite of the attractiveness of the thinking of Xenophanes,
Heraclitus and the Pythagoreans to Plato, there can be no doubt
that of all the Presocratics it was Parmenides who left the deepest
impression on his mind. The dichotomy of the way of seeming
and the way of true being reappears in Plato: the separation of the
two worlds seemed to Aristotle to be the deplorably distinctive
mark of Plato's thought. The fact that Plato named a dialogue
after Parmenides does not necessarily guarantee respect, but he
does refer to him as 'a man to inspire reverence, an awesome figure', and it is surely not without significance that the most severe
testing of Plato's mature theory of Forms is put into the mouth of
Parmenides. That testing ends with a paternal admonition to a
young Socrates (who would have stood for other young men in
the Academic in the 370s BC and afterwards) that however great
the apparent difficulties in the theory might be, 'if ... a man refuses
to admit that Forms of things exist or to distinguish a definite
Form in every case, he will have nothing on which to fix his
thought, so long as he will not allow that each thing has a character which is always the same; and in so doing he will completely
destroy the significance of all discourse.' (*Parm.* 135B. C Cornford's trs.)[3] The comment is particularly interesting in view of the
close relationship which can be found in Plato's thought between
the Forms and God.

The supreme indication of Plato's admiration for Parmenides
is, however, the note of triumph in his voice when he finally sees a
way around the arguments against negative statements and
change which had been produced by Parmenides and which had
put his predecessors, Empedocles and Anaxagoras, to such lab-
orious rounds to evade. That can be heard in the passage in the

Sophist where he says: 'We shall find it necessary in self-defence to put to the question that pronouncement of father Parmenides, and establish by main force that what is not, in some respect has being, and conversely that what is, in a way is not.' Theaetetus agrees: 'It is plain that the course of the argument requires us to maintain that at all costs.' 'Plain enough for the blind to see', says the Stranger. 'We must now dare to lay unfilial hands on that pronouncement.' (241D 242A) Plato was well aware that it was no easy task to rebut Parmenides, and his efforts to do so had obviously caused him to think deeply about his own theories concerning the unchanging nature of reality. 'Possibly ... our minds are in the same state of confusion about reality (as they are unreality). We profess to be quite at our ease about the real and to understand the word when it is spoken, ... when perhaps we are equally in the dark about both.' (243C) Plato demonstrates in the closely reasoned section that follows that confusion is certainly not his normal state of mind, and after dealing with the materialists turns to the 'Friends of the Forms'. He asks: 'Are we really to be so easily convinced that change, life, soul, understanding have no place in that which is perfectly real?' And then, 'if it has intelligence, life, and soul, can we say that a living thing remains at rest in complete changelessness?'(248E 249A) Consequently, 'it seems that only one course is open to the philosopher who values knowledge and the rest above all else. He must refuse to accept from the champions either of the One or of the many Forms the doctrine that all Reality is changeless ... he must declare that Reality or the sum of things is both at once all that is unchangeable and all that is in change.' (249C D)

The passage just quoted has been much debated. It appears to me that we are being presented with a well-marked change in Plato's own thought, and that in it we have a remarkable concession to a new vision of the nature of reality which he now sees clearly must exist along with the reality of Parmenides which was itself for him so important. If this be the case, it raises another intriguing question: What did Aristotle think of this change of heart in Plato, or, what notice did he take of it in his theories about the Unmoved Mover(s)?

That question we shall examine later: to end this chapter we turn to the final influence on Plato mentioned by Aristotle. This is Socrates. The inspiration that Socrates provided for Plato's life is, I think, too obvious to need arguing. Once again, Aristotle's report is well known: 'Socrates ... was busying himself about ethical matters and neglecting the world of nature as a whole but seeking the universal in these ethical matters, and fixed thought for the first time on definitions.' Aristotle continues: 'Plato accepted his teaching, but because of the Heraclitean influence mentioned above turned the quest away from sensible things and on to entities of another kind; for the common definition could not be a definition of any sensible thing, as they were always changing. Things of this sort, then, he called Forms, and sensible things, he said, were all named after these, and in virtue of a relation to these; for the many existed by participation in the Forms that have the same name as they.' (Met. 987b1 10) This account of the difference between Socrates and Plato would, I think, be generally accepted nowadays (whatever about the summary of the theory of Forms). Slightly more disputed is the extent of Socrates' direct influence on Plato as regards specifically theological thought. (I emphasise 'direct' and 'specifically theological', because, as we shall see, any influence bearing on the Theory of Forms implies indirect, if complicated, influence on Plato's theology.) But the direct influence is, I think, considerable. One can hardly read Plato's *Apology*, Socrates defence when on trial for his life, and not come away with the impression of Socrates as a deeply religious man, however difficult it may be to give the right meaning to what he refers to as 'the god' or 'God'. The *Apology* is only one early witness. *Alcibiades* is another clear one. There (133Cff) Plato's Socrates talks of how the soul resembles God because of knowledge and thought. God is the mirror of what is best in us, and by knowing Him we will know ourselves – an idea that was to have a very long history.[2] Moreover, the very simplicity of Xenophon's account of Socrates' 'theology' seems to put its authenticity beyond doubt. Moral idealism based on religious fervour was to become the hallmark of Plato's thought, more obviously perhaps than it was that of Socrates, but that Socrates was the most important theological influence on Plato, emotionally and intellectually, should not be doubted.

Finally, Socrates was frequently accused of being a Sophist, a mercenary intellectual with theories on everything in heaven and earth. This is one of the unstated charges which he tried to rebut in his speech in his own defence. To some people being a sophist meant being either an agnostic about the existence of the gods, as Protagoras could have been accused of being, or an atheist. In the *Apology*, according to Plato, Socrates tells an accuser that he is being confused with Anaxagoras (who had died about thirty years before this). Socrates says that Anaxagoras' views on the nondivinity of the sun and the moon are not his. But we can also believe the report in the *Phaedo* that Socrates was excited by Anaxagoras' theories of *nous* or Mind and its governance of the world. The notion of a divine mind and its care for the universe was popular in fifth century Athens:[3] we can imagine how these ideas would have been discussed in the circle of Socrates to which Plato belonged, and how Plato would have been stimulated by them to develop his own theories which he expounds in Book Ten of the *Laws*. The priority of soul to body, which was a central element in the moral teaching of Socrates, was to become a most important part of all succeeding theorising on theology. This priority, in Plato's eyes, was in itself a sufficient bastion against any sophistic agnosticism or atheism. But Plato's vehemence on these matters is an indication of how the free speculation of Athens, which culminated in the sophistic movement, stimulated him in the development of his own theories in theology.

CHAPTER TWO

Plato

The notion of Eros, loving desire, is central to the philosophy of Plato. It appears throughout the dialogues, notably in the *Phaedrus* (esp. 249Eff), but is expounded most fully in the symposium. There it is made clear that eros runs right through the universe, and affects all forms of being. But the highest form of eros is the desire of wisdom. The goal of this desire is the vision of the beautiful; the attainment of this vision will result in the perfect virtue, through which a man will be called the friend of god and will become immortal insofar as that is possible for man. (212A) The vision is attained by a gradual ascent, and a turning away from the lesser beauties which distract one from the higher. Socrates, the personification of eros and of the 'philosophos', lover of wisdom, is portrayed as superior to all temptations, including sexual love, which might turn him from the vision of the beautiful. Yet he professes himself knowledgeable only about questions of love, eros. (177D) Eros, then, in the highest sense should refer to the preoccupation of Socrates, manifested throughout the dialogues, with moral questions, the consciousness of the lack of the virtue which we should have, and the concern to make the soul as good as possible.

This activity is referred to in the *Theaetetus* (i) as *homoiosis theo*, becoming like to god. Socrates says: 'Evils, Theodorus, can never be done away with, for the good must always have its contrary; but they have no place in the divine world, even though they must haunt this region of our mortal nature. That is why we should make all speed to take flight from this world to the other, and that means becoming like the divine so far as we can, and that again is to become righteous with the help of wisdom ... In the divine there is no shadow of unrighteousness, only the perfection of righteousness, and nothing is more like the divine than any one of us who becomes as righteous as possible.' (176A C)

The context of this passage is Socrates' praise of philosophy, at the end of which Theodorus has said: 'If you could convince everyone, Socrates, as you convince me, there would be more peace and fewer evils in the world.' (176A) Socrates replies in the words quoted above, and in the reply there is a remarkable emphasis on the fact that the divine world is perfect and that evil has no place there. Nevertheless, Plato has been called a dualist because of other passages in his writings, and some would go so far as to say that in the ultimate analysis Plato explicitly admits the existence of two different principles on which the world depends.

Dualism seems to be explicitly rejected in some important middle to later dialogues: it is the latest dialogues, especially the *Timaeus* and the *Laws* which cause most trouble. For Plato's rejection of dualism we can look to the *Republic* and the *Statesman*. He says in the *Republic*: 'For the good we must assume no other cause than God, but the cause of evil we must look for in other things and not in God' (379C) and he goes on to attack Homer for suggesting that Zeus is the dispenser of evil. To round off all this discussion he emphatically repeats that a basic principle about the gods which the poets will have to accept is 'that God is not the cause of all things, but only of the good.' (380C) Again in the *Statesman* he says: 'We may not say that a pair of divinities make it (the Universe) revolve alternately in opposed senses because the mind of the one God is contrary to the mind of the other.' (269E) Yet in both these cases of rejection of dualism there is the admission of the existence of a problem. That becomes even more obvious in the *Timaeus*.

In the *Timaeus* the *demiourgos*, or maker, who is good, does not seem to have things entirely his own way. He is confronted with the intractability of 'matter'. *Timaeus* says, in a passage that was to be referred to time and time again in succeeding centuries on the overflowing goodness of God: 'Let me tell you then why the maker made this world of change. He was good, and the good can never have any jealousy of anything. And being free from jealousy, he desired that all things should be as like himself as they could be. This is in the truest sense the origin of creation and of the world ... God desired that all things should be good and nothing bad, so far as this was attainable. And so finding the whole visible sphere not at rest, but moving in an irregular and disorderly fashion, out of disorder he brought order, considering that this was in every way better than the other.' (29D 30A) Somewhat later 'so far as was attainable' in the passage above is made a little more specific: 'Thus far in what we have been saying, with small exceptions, the works of intelligence have been set forth, and now we must place by the side of them in our discourse the things which come into being through necessity, for the fashioning of this world is the combined work of necessity and mind. Mind, the ruling power, persuaded necessity to bring the greater part of the things that come into being to perfection, and so and after this manner in the beginning, through necessity made subject to reason, this universe was created.' (47E 48A) The nature of necessity is not explained in any satisfactory way. Yet it must be a considerable force. *Timaeus* says in 56C: 'The ratios of the numbers, motions, and other properties of elemental forms everywhere God has exactly perfected and harmonised in due proportion, as far as *necessity* was willing or was persuaded.' (My italics)

A possible explanation of the problem of evil may be proferred in the *Timaeus* with the statement that the maker handed over the formation of the three kinds of mortal beings to the gods who have come into being. (41Aff) 'Of the divine he himself was the maker, but the making of the mortal he committed to his offspring.' (69C) He did this 'that he might be guiltless of future evil.' (42D) Unsatisfactory as this is as an explanation, there can be no doubt that the tendency of the dialogue is still simply to insist that a good God is in charge of the world and that evil is merely incidental. The *Laws*, the last big work of Plato, has a somewhat different approach. Book Ten of that work opens with a discussion of offences against the gods and it is in the course of that discussion that the question of the source of evil is mentioned. Some offenders against the gods, it is said, fall into error because of a theory concerning what is primary. They think 'that fire and water, earth and air, are the most primitive origins of all things … and that the soul is a late derivative from them.' (891c) The truth is that soul 'is among the primal things, elder-born than all bodies and prime source of all their changes and transformations … if we can show that soul came first – that it was not fire, nor air, but soul which was there to begin with – it will be perfectly true to say that it is the existence of soul which is most eminently natural.' (892A C) The *Athenian* attempts to show the priority of soul through an examination of motion. In the course of this passage, soul is shown to be the first of all things because its nature and definition is 'self-moving motion.' (896A) So, the *Athenian* says, we must agree that 'soul is the cause of good and evil, fair and foul, right and wrong – in fact of all contraries, if we mean to assert it as the universal cause.' (896C) It controls heaven itself. The *Athenian* emphasises that we must assume that there are at least two souls in charge, one which does good and one which is capable of the contrary. (896E) All goes well when soul is accompanied by wisdom, and badly if accompanied by foolishness. The *Athenian* is not specific about the extent of the spheres of influence of wisdom and foolishness in the world, but he and Clinias (and, we may presume, Megillus) are convinced, particularly from the order in the universe (898C), that the supremely good soul is in charge of the universe and does not neglect anything, however small. 'Our king' has so ordered things throughout the universe that virtue will triumph, even though individuals are free to do evil, and it is conceded that bad things seem to be numerous in the universe. (906A)

I think we should conclude from this that talk of dualism is misplaced. Plato was primarily concerned, as so often, with defeating the materialists, and thought he had done so when he established the priority of soul. After that, he felt, all things would fall into their proper order, and among them evil would take its place. Human freedom will take a large share of the responsibility for evil in the universe. The notion will recur frequently in the course of this work.

Finally we should mention that there is, besides the written work, a report of unwritten teaching by Plato.[2] Some would maintain that here also two principles were pitted one against the other. But in spite of Aristotle we must, I think, consider the case not proven. Plato was either not a strict dualist or if he was he did not make himself clear. With that we must leave the question.

We have seen that for Plato it is love that binds the universe together, and we have seen how, because of this love, man wishes to flee the world and its associated evils and come to God. It is obvious that in Plato's eyes man has such a relationship with God and must remain aware of it. But what about God? Plato maintains, as one would expect many of his contemporaries would also have held, that the gods are concerned with men (see the remarks of Cephalus in *Republic* 330D and of Adimantus in 363C E). Throughout the dialogues, from the *Apology* to the *Laws*, he insists that the gods are concerned that man shall do good and avoid evil, and that man shall be rewarded or punished by them in an afterlife in accordance with his behaviour in this life. Nowhere is this concern of the gods more obvious than in the *Phaedo*.

The *Phaedo* is regarded by many as Plato's masterpiece, and from the start was greatly admired for its loving portrait of Socrates on his last day. The fate of Socrates gave a weight to Plato's arguments for the immortality of the soul which they do not merit in themselves, and it also gave a popularity to the dialogue itself which ensured that the views of the relations between gods and men contained in it were well-known in the ancient and early

Christian world. Socrates tells his friends not to grieve at his death: death is a reward from God to those who have purified themselves enough to merit the soul's deliverance from the body. (67A) Universal justice demands reward for the pure and exclusion from the company of the blessed for those who are not pure. (67B) Socrates feels that he is going into the presence of the god and can therefore sing his swan-song of happiness. (85A b) He had said in the *Apology*: 'Nothing can harm a good man either in life or after death, and his fortunes are not a matter of indifference to the gods.' (41C D) He repeats this profession of faith in God's protection in the *Phaedo*: 'God is our keeper and we are his possessions.' (62C D) We are in the service of the gods and they are 'the very best of masters', wise and supremely good. (62D, 63C) Plato repeats throughout the dialogues his belief that the good man is dear to the gods who will never neglect him (see, for example, *Rep.* 613A, *Philebus* 39E), and he reiterates his confidence that justice demands reward and punishment in an afterlife. The great eschatological myths of the *Gorgias*, the *Phaedo* and the *Republic* bear eloquent witness to the same conviction. As he says at the end of the *Republic*: 'If we are guided by me we shall believe that the soul is immortal and capable of enduring all extremes of good and evil, and so we shall hold ever to the upward way and pursue righteousness with wisdom always and ever, that we may be dear to ourselves and to the gods both during our sojourn here and when we receive our reward.' (621C)

Yet all this emphasis on the gods' concern with man sits rather uneasily with another deeply held conviction of Plato: the insignificance of man. This conviction appears most clearly in a famous passage in the *Laws* which we shall quote in a moment, but it is not confined to that rather pessimistic work. It is implicit in the story of Socrates' realisation of what his wisdom consisted in and in his interpretation of the oracle which guided him to the following conclusion: 'The truth of the matter, gentlemen, is pretty certainly this, that real wisdom is the property of God, and this oracle is his way of telling us that human wisdom has little or no value.' (*Apology* 23A) The mockery that Plato pours on Protagoras' dictum that 'man is the measure of all things' in the *Theaetetus* is prompted partly by a rather low opinion of man. In the *Laws* he says: 'We may imagine that each of us living creatures is a puppet made by gods, possibly as a plaything, or possibly with some more serious purpose.' (644D) He repeats this image later: 'While God is the real goal of all beneficent serious endeavour, man, as we said before, has been constructed as a toy for God, and this is, in fact, the finest thing about him.' (803C) It is in this context that he says: 'To be sure, man's life is a business which does not deserve to be taken too seriously; yet we cannot help being in earnest with it, and there's the pity. Still, as we are here in this world, no doubt for us the becoming thing is to show this earnestness in a suitable way.' (803B) Therefore, men 'are to play their play, win heaven's favour for it, and so live out their lives as what they really are – puppets in the main, though with some touch of reality about them, too.' (804B) At this Megillus understandably remarks: 'I must say, sir, you have a low estimate of human beings.' The Athenian replies: 'Do not be amazed by that, Megillus. Bear with me. I had God before my mind's eye, and felt myself to be what I have just said. However, if you will have it so, man shall be something not so insignificant but more serious.' (804B)

On the face of it, such an attitude would not appear to leave much room for a relationship as a Christian might understand it between God and man, and certainly it would appear to leave very little room for moral responsibility on man's part if he is a puppet controlled by strings. And yet in the *Laws* also Plato announces as the basic principle of his new state that 'God is the measure of all things', and man's salvation lies in becoming like to God by practice of the virtues, and in praying to and worshipping God. And he says that the man who in this way becomes like to God 'is loved by God'. (716) It is impiety, as he says in Book Ten, not only to believe that there are no gods, but also to believe that they do not care for men. Moreover, in spite of the puppet language, Plato's system asserts throughout man's moral responsibility. This is presented most impressively in the myth of the Republic where we are given the words of Lachesis to the souls that are to start a new life: 'Souls that live for a day, now is the beginning of another cycle of mortal generation where birth is the beacon of death. No divinity shall cast lots for you, but you shall choose your own deity. Let him to whom falls the first lot first select a life to which he shall cleave of necessity. Virtue has no master above her, and each shall have more or less of her as he honours or dishonours her. The blame is his who chooses. God is blameless.' (617d e)

Man must live up to a standard set by the gods themselves. Plato is scandalised by the suggestion that gods might act immorally. God is good in reality and always to be spoken of as such. (*Rep.* 379b) But once again we are confronted with a difficulty when we try to visualise how man can imitate or become like unto God. We meet another of the antitheses which are so frequent in Plato's thought. It is very difficult for man even to conceive of the deity on which he is to model himself. God is good, and yet when Plato comes to describe essential goodness in the *Republic* he begins by confessing his inability to give anything like an adequate picture. 'Let us give up asking for the present what the good is in itself: I'm afraid a satisfactory answer is beyond the scope of our present inquiry. But I will tell you, if you like, about something which I imagine to be a child of the good, and to resemble it very closely.' (506d e) He then goes on to illustrate the nature of the good by the analogy of the sun, but he keeps emphasising that he cannot show what the good is in itself. Finally he says: 'This reality that gives their truth to the objects or knowledge and the power of knowing to the knower, you must say is the idea of good, and you must conceive it as being the cause of knowledge and of truth in so far as known. Yet beautiful as knowledge and truth are, you must think of the good being more beautiful than either of these.' (508d 509a) The good is higher than all things: all things owe their being to it, and yet 'the good itself is not being, but is beyond being and superior to it in dignity and power.' (509b)

This famous sentence, and the phrase *epekeina tés ousias*, beyond being, was taken by some later thinkers as applied directly to God, not just the good, by Plato, and was seized on eagerly by those who wished to emphasise God's transcendence. It might in fact be called the charter of the later negative theology.[3] Phrases could also be taken from the Parmenides to support this interpretation, and particularly from the so-called *First Hypothesis*. 'It appears that the One neither is one nor is at all ... It is not named or spoken of, not an object of opinion or of knowledge, not perceived by any creature.' (Parmenides 141e 142a) The One and the good were assimilated. The result was that, despite the ordinary connotations of 'goodness', these forms of expression about God drew attention primarily to his immense distance from man. Two views of God had to be reconciled as a consequence: God as utterly transcendent and remote, in this interpretation, and God as close to man, the 'good' God ultimately responsible for man and caring for him.

This clash of views appears in Plato, not just in particular isolated statements or in different conceptions of God's activity, but in the general presentation of God that emerges from the dialogues. Plato's reflections on the divinity are shaped by two traditions. One is the presentation of the deity in the personal, and sometimes all too human, terms of Greek religion. The other is the tradition of Presocratic philosophy where the ultimate is presented

as a principle and is at the same time hymned in words that seem
to us more fitting to a person. Plato combines and blends both
these traditions, and as a result he is taken at times to be talking
about God in language that would be more suited to a principle.
God is assimilated to the forms rather than to Zeus, let us say. We
may say that God is perfection, truth, goodness and so on, and it
seems quite natural. In the same way the highest forms of the dialogues seem to become personified. Plato represents them as exercising an attraction and taking on a quasi-personal appeal. So, for
example, in the *Symposium* the vision of beauty is described in
terms which St Augustine could easily have adopted for his vision of God in the *Confessions*, and they are terms which Dionysius seems to be deliberately echoing in the divine names as we
shall see. 'It is an everlasting loveliness which neither comes nor
goes, which neither flowers nor fades, for such beauty is the same
on every hand, the same then as now, here as there, this way as
that way, the same to every worshipper as it is to every other ...
Subsisting of itself and by itself in an eternal oneness, while every
lovely thing partakes of it in such sort that, however much the
parts may wax and wane, it will be neither more nor less, but still
the same inviolable whole.' (Symp. 211a b)

Similarly, the sun in the *Phaedo* is described as 'contemplat-
ing the true and divine and unconjecturable, and drawing inspiration from it.' (84a) The philosophers in the *Republic* will have
seen 'the reality of the beautiful, the just and the good' (520c), just
as the soul in the *Phaedrus* comes to the region where 'true beauty
dwells, without colour or shape, that cannot be touched; reason
alone, the soul's pilot, can behold it, and all true knowledge is
knowledge thereof.' (247c) We may take one final example from
the sophist. There is the sophist is contrasted with the philosopher,
and of him it is said: 'The philosopher, whose thoughts constantly
dwell upon the nature of reality, is difficult to see because his
region is so bright, for the eye of the vulgar soul cannot endure to
keep its gaze fixed on the divine.' (254a b)

Statements like these were often taken by later thinkers to be
statements about God, and indeed it has been suggested that later
Platonism drew up a kind of anthology of favourite texts to illustrate Plato's theology. But the texts quoted are very often statements about forms or principles rather than about a person. The
element of remoteness and impersonality which is introduced in
this way is increased by another feature in Plato's thought to
which we must now turn our attention, and that is Plato's emphasis on the unchanging nature of the highest realities. We can

see this in the passage from the *Symposium* which we have just quoted, and it is understandable that there should be such an emphasis on the unchanging nature of forms in a philosophy which was evolved in an attempt to provide the moral convictions derived from Socrates in particular with an unshakable metaphysical basis. But Plato is also wary of social change and of the instability and fickleness, as he thinks, of the character of the man who provokes such change. This, and the powerful influence of Parmenides, produce reasoning such as the following in the *Republic*: 'Do you think that God is a wizard and capable of manifesting himself by design, now in one aspect, now in another, at one time himself changing and altering his shape in many transformations and at another deceiving us and causing us to believe such things about him, or that he is simple and less likely than anything else to depart from his own form? ... Is it not true that to be altered and moved by something else happens least to things that are in the best condition? ... But God, surely, and everything that belongs to God, is in every way in the best possible state ... Then does he change himself for the better and to something fairer, or for the worse and to something uglier than himself?' Neither alternative is to be contemplated, and the conclusion follows: 'It is impossible then even for a god to wish to alter himself, but, as it appears, each of them, being the fairest and best possible, abides forever simply in his own form.' (380d 381c)

Similarly Plato says in the *Statesman* that 'ever to be the same, steadfast and abiding, is the prerogative of divine things only.' (269d) But perhaps we are justified in thinking that here and in *Philebus* 58-59 Plato has in mind the principle rather than the personal element in 'the divine'. For in the *Sophist* he has introduced a very important modification of his thinking about the unchanging nature of the perfect, as we saw in the previous chapter when talking about Parmenides. There, in *Sophist* 248, he turns to 'the friends of the forms'. It is accepted that, according to them, 'real being is always in the same unchanging state, whereas becoming is variable'. They will also hold that 'a power of acting and being acted upon belongs to becoming, but neither of these powers is compatible with real being'. But this position contains difficulties because of the process of knowing, and the Stranger, who in this dialogue plays the role normally taken by Socrates, bursts out: 'But tell me, in heaven's name, are we really to be so easily convinced that change, life, soul, understanding have no place in that which is perfectly real – that it has neither life nor thought, but stands immutable in solemn aloofness, devoid of intelligence?'

(249a) Theaetetus agrees that this would be very strange indeed. Apparently, then, the philosopher 'must refuse to accept from the champions either of the one or many forms the doctrine that all reality is changeless, and he must turn a deaf ear to the other party who represent reality as everywhere changing. Like a child begging for 'both', he must declare that reality or the sum of things is both at once – all that is unchangeable and all that is in change.' (249c d)

Reality, as Plato goes on to point out, is a very difficult concept indeed. Fixity in the universe is required for intelligibility, but from that one may not argue that the perfectly static is the perfect intelligence or perfectly intelligible. Plato had obviously been bothered with the question for some time. He had raised the difficulty of our knowledge of the forms among the objections to them which he formulates in the first part of the Parmenides. (134) Even more interestingly he continued with an objection to the gods knowing our world. The gods are to be confined to their own perfection. A similar type of difficulty was to be raised later on in connection with the Christian God's knowledge of the world and the Christian doctrine of creation. Both these difficulties were connected with the notion of the unchanging nature of perfection which we saw Plato putting forward in the *Republic* and elsewhere. In Plato's own references to creation he is not, as far as we can see, bothered by any such considerations. But the doctrine of the unchanging nature of perfection was, through Aristotle, to raise the greatest problems in the theology of God's relation to the world.

Any mention of Plato and creation brings up immediately the *Timaeus*, one of the last of his writings and famous throughout the centuries even when Greek was largely lost to the West because it had been translated into Latin. It is a story about 'the origin of the cosmic system', and one of the first statements made is that the world has not always existed but has started from some beginning.' (28) This statement was the subject of much debate by later commentators on Plato: did he mean literally creation in time?[6] (As with so many questions in Plato, one cannot with assurance answer simply yes or no). He then warns: 'To discover the maker and father of this universe is indeed a hard task, and having found him it would be impossible to tell everyone about him.' (28e) It was tempting and easy for some people later to say that Plato was anticipating the Christian God who made and cared for the universe. Plato was of course concerned to emphasise divine providence, but as an anticipation of the Christian God, his maker or *demiourgos* of the *Timaeus* is subject to some qualifications. First-ly, he does not seem to be in absolute control of his material, but does his best with what is given him. (31b, 37d) Secondly, he looks to the ideal pattern (28a, 29a, 39e), but it is not said that he created it. His task is to realise the pattern as perfectly as possible in the material, and the material apparently lets itself be 'persuaded'. (48a, 56c)

What cannot be doubted, however, in the *Timaeus* or elsewhere in Plato's writings is the primacy of soul or spirit over matter. Taking up a theme of the *Phaedrus* (245 6), he says in the *Laws*, the last of his work, that soul is 'self initiating motion' (896a) or the source of motion. So it is superior to body (which is moved with-out being source of motion), and must rule the body. He goes on from this to argue that one must believe in the gods and that these gods care for mankind. And whatever difficulties there may be in reconciling Plato's statements on the soul throughout his works, one thing is constant, that it is through the soul that we are related to the divine. The likening to God, which is the aim of existence, is a likening of the soul to God; the body is to be left behind. The mes-sage of the *Apology* at the beginning of his career is essentially the same as that of the *Laws* at the end. Aristotle was to be critical of the expression of Plato's views on motion (*Physics* 8, 5), but they con-tributed largely to the formation of his own theory. For much else in regard to the soul Aristotle drew on Plato, and nowhere more than in his statements on the necessity of 'putting on immortality'. It is the immortal union of the soul with God that Plato is primarily concerned with, and it is fundamental to his philosophy.

We shall be seeing something more on mind and soul in Plato in the next chapter. We may conclude this chapter on his theology with two quotations from late works which show both his convict-ion of the importance of the subject and his awareness of our limit-ations in our knowledge of it. Firstly, its importance: 'Surely one of the finest fields of knowledge is theology .... It's supremely im-portant to appreciate – so far as it's given to man to know these things – the existence of the gods and the obvious extent of their power.' (*Laws* 966c) But, finally, our limitations: 'Don't be sur-prised, Socrates, if on many matters concerning the gods and the whole world of change, we are unable in every respect and on every occasion to render a consistent and accurate account. You must be satisfied if our account is as likely as any, remembering that both you and I who are sitting on judgment on it are merely human, and should not look for anything more than a likely story in such matters.' (*Timaeus* 29)

It is wrong to ask: 'What is Plato's final answer to the God-problem?' There are more questions than answers in Plato on the matter. But the questions always imply that an answer is to be found, and the centuries that followed were stimulated to supply answers from his work because of his own evident conviction that answers existed, even though he had carefully avoided giving any. The results are occasionally astonishing, to some scholars at any rate, not the least of these being the theological treatment we have referred to above, given to the second half of Plato's *Parmenides* where he deals with the notion of 'One'. Dodds has, however, demonstrated how the negative theology could be read into the first hypothesis of the *Parmenides* (137 142), and how the form of the good of the *Republic* could be linked to the One of the *Parmenides* as 'beyond being'. We have to see apparent extravagances in context, and the context was a world which, while still pagan, saw Plato not as the philosopher but as the theologian par excellence.

CHAPTER THREE

Aristotle

The theology of Aristotle has achieved any prominence it has in this century mainly because of the debate, associated particularly with the name of Jaeger, concerning the relative chronology of his writings. Were it not for this debate, the ordinary student of Aristotle might be forgiven for thinking that Aristotle had no interest in theology at all. This is understandable: Aristotle was interested in so many more tractable problems that it is easy either to pay little attention to his theology or to describe it as, for instance, Hartshorne did, as being concerned with 'a divine aristocrat ... Serenely indifferent to the world's turmoil.'[1]

That, however, should not be taken to mean that Aristotle has no time for the notion of God or gods. His theological system is certainly austere, but his general attitude to divinity is human enough. Chroust is an enthusiastic expounder of the 'pious' Aristotle, and writes, for instance: 'The *On Prayer* ... Is an eloquent example of Aristotle's basic religious convictions, declaratory of his piety'.[2] But even if we are apprehensive about claiming so much about Aristotle, and particularly on the basis of the lost works, we can still see from the main corpus that a theology of some sort would have been part of the furniture of Aristotle's mind. Or, as he says himself: 'All human beings have an opinion about God.' (*De Caelo* 270b5 6)

The insistence that Aristotle had a theology may seem a misplaced labouring of a fairly obvious point. But the notion which Jaeger did so much to popularise, the notion that Aristotle the empiricist ultimately overcame Aristotle the metaphysician, that Aristotle became himself rather than a Platonist, still needs to be opposed.[3] One may, if one wishes, assert that Aristotle is not always consistent in his thinking. But rather than judge him from this superhuman height, it is better to accept that in his theology, as elsewhere, there were, and remain, different strands in Aristotle's thought, strands which were on occasion woven together, however various they were and whatever the outcome for an ideal consistency. It is Book Lambda (Twelve) of the *Metaphysics* that we shall chiefly be concerned with, and this appears to Elders, for instance, as 'a splendid synthesis of *Academic* theories which are transferred on a new level.' (my italics)[4] We sometimes find in Aristotle something other than what our prejudices would have led us to expect. It is better to accept the apparent facts than bend them to fit our theories. Aristotle may indeed appear for the most part the patient pedant for whom Bertrand Russell had so little regard. But there is another point of view, best expressed by Guthrie: 'Cornford spoke of "the idea of aspiration" as a common feature of the philosophies of Socrates, Plato and Aristotle ... It is in Aristotle that "the philosophy of aspiration" finds its culmination.'[5]

After this introduction, we may now turn to the theological section of Book Lambda of the *Metaphysics*. In chapter six of that book Aristotle begins his discussion of indestructible being. He starts from his familiar position that substances, or entities, are the primary forms of being. (He means, for instance, that before one can speak of someone being tall, or pale, or the brother of x, there must be some one there to be talked about: he is the entity who happens to be tall, pale etc.) He argues that there must be some indestructible entities, for if there were not, all things would be destructible. But everything cannot be destructible, because that would mean eventually that there would be no realities which move, and no time in which they move. But it is inconceivable that movement should not exist. If this were the case, if there were no movement, on Aristotle's supposition that whatever actually changes must first have been capable of being changed, when change did actually occur, there would have had to be a movement beforehand to account for the actual change. Similarly, if movement were destructible, one would have to envisage a sequence of changes and then no change. But this in itself would be a change in the sequence: therefore you would have a change after the last change.

These would seem to have been Aristotle's reasons for considering movement indestructible: they are not spelt out in chapter six. He says that time also must be indestructible 'for there could not be a before and after if there were not time.' (1071b8 9) Once again he does not spell out his reasons for this statement, but drawing on the other parts of the corpus we may suppose that his reasoning was as follows: time exists as a continuum of 'nows'. Each 'now' is both the end of the past and the beginning of the future. So of no 'now' can it be said that it is the end one of all or the beginning of all.

Then he says that time and movement are either identical or that one goes with the other, and since time is a continuum, movement also is, without beginning or end. This is local movement, movement in a place, and, more exactly movement in a circle. This opening section of chapter six on the existence of indestructible entities, based on the indestructibility of time and change, presupposes an acceptance of some basic Aristotelian concepts and, as we saw, draws on arguments from other parts of the corpus. These concepts and arguments have occasioned much discussion and disagreement: even a reading of the brief account here given makes it abundantly clear why there should be such disagreement. But we need not concern ourselves with that for the moment, and, besides, all this is meant only as an introduction to the main part of this chapter which is devoted to the explanation of movement. Here (1071b12 1072a18) he argues that there must be a principle whose very nature it is always to be in action. There is no use in having a) something which is capable of being in action, but is not actually in action, or b) something which is actually in action at a particular moment, but is capable of not being in action. For then either a), we shall not have movement, or, b) there is the possibility (and we might add, the danger) that we shall not. But it has already been established that there must always be movement. Therefore there must be a principle whose very nature it is to be always in action.

Aristotle then turns in chapter seven to consider how such a principle could exist and could operate. There must be a principle whose very nature it is to be always actually in action, for we have seen that there is always movement (and this movement is circular, for reasons which he does not here explain), and so, he says, the first heaven must be eternal. This is the heaven in which stars are fixed. (Aristotle is again taking knowledge of his teaching elsewhere for granted.) This heaven can be seen to be always moving round and round, and whatever is moving this is the eternal reality which is always actually in action. Just here, at this key point in the argument, the Greek text has obviously been corrupted, but Aristotle seems to be saying that the first heaven is responsible for all the movement in the world, but it itself is being moved by the first principle, which does not itself need to be and is not moved at any time: it is always in action. But what can we suggest which would act in such a way, i.e. move or cause change without itself being moved or being changed? It must be something different from ordinary physical action and reaction. But, Aristotle says, there is something in our experience which causes change or movement without being changed. Objects of desire and of thought cause change or movement in such a way. (Aristotle does not give examples, but we may illustrate crudely what he meant. The face that launched a thousand ships is not reported to have been moved by the event. The problem of evil provokes thought, but it still remains, unchanged, while the ink splashes around it.) And in fact, as Aristotle further points out, it will be found that at the very highest level what most attracts desire and what most engages thought coincide. Mind (or *nous*) is moved, or thought is engaged by, the entity or reality which is always exercising its full power and attraction, and is not dependent on other factors, is not composite. Desire follows what it knows to be good. And consequently this supremely good being, through being desired, causes all things to move through its influence on the first heaven; on it the world depends.

Immediately, however, Aristotle emphasises that, even though it causes change and movement, it is not itself changed or moved. The reasons for this have already been given in chapter six. Yet it is always in action, and Aristotle now attempts to explain what this action is which is neither change nor movement. He uses analogies from the life of human beings. Firstly (1072b10) we would like to be free from any necessity to be other than what we are, and the first being is not subject to any outside pressures. Secondly, and positively, if we were free from limitations, what would be the best life? This will be the life which the first being leads. Aristotle says that we humans can only live the best type of life for short stretches at a time. It emerges from other contexts that this *diagóge*, as he calls it, is philosophical contemplation. This is the activity that gives us pleasure, but of course we tire because of our deficiencies, whereas the first being never does. The most concentrated and purest thought is concerned with the perfect object. But the first being is perfection, so that it is the object of its own thought.

God's life, then, is one of everlasting contemplation (*theória*); contemplation is the best thing in our lives and that which gives most pleasure, and in God it is even more wonderful, for it goes on forever. (Aristotle's Greek indicates that the wonder exceeds our comprehension.) And we talk properly of God's life, for life is activity, and the mind in action is life, and God is that mind in action in the highest sense, life perfect and eternal. Aristotle is insistent that God is a living being, the best living life, who not only has, but is, perpetual life. And, after a brief passing criticism of views which might seem to be at variance with his, he summarises the chapter, saying that it is clear that there is a being which is eternal and unmoving and separate from sensible things. He also says that it has been shown (although it is not clear that it has) that this being must be without magnitude, and, once again, that it is not subject to influence or change.

Chapter eight of Book Lambda, on the number of eternal moving principles, has caused a great deal of debate, but we may leave it to one side, because whatever else was to pass into Christian theology from Greek philosophy, there was no likelihood that Christians were going to accept twenty-six or thirty-three or fifty-five or forty-seven gods. Besides, as Elders says, 'There are serious difficulties which make it doubtful whether the chapter, as it now is, was written by Aristotle himself.'[6] I move on to chapter nine, which can be taken as the logical successor to chapter seven. In this chapter, Aristotle, as is frequently his fashion, raises objections to the position he has outlined in chapter seven. The functioning of mind, *nous*, raises some difficulties. There appears to be a dilemma: if it thinks of nothing, it is no better than someone asleep, but, on the other hand, if it has an object of thought it would appear to be dominated by this and to be inferior to the object. It is assumed that divine thinking will be something better than mere sleeping, so the only question that remains is, how can the divine mind be saved from being dependent on something inferior to itself? In a sense, Aristotle is simply working out in detail what he has already stated in chapter seven about the first being as the object of its own thought. So he states the alternatives: the divine *nous* thinks either of itself or something else. If of something else, this something else is either always the same or something different. Obviously, some objects are not worthy of its thought: it must think only of the highest, and never change from this, because change could only be for the worse. (We recall the same line of thinking in Plato.) It thinks therefore of itself, or rather it thinks itself: Aristotle deliberately emphasises the unbroken activity of the divine mind by repeating the verbal form of the noun – 'the thinking is the thinking of thinking'.

But immediately Aristotle raises more difficulties for himself. Knowledge, he says, generally seems to be concerned with an outside object and with itself only incidentally. What about the divine *nous*, then? Why is it different? Secondly, it is one thing to think and another to be thought: through which process is it to be said that *nous* attains its happiness, seeing that it is here both thinking and being thought? His answer to the first difficulty is that in some cases the act of thinking is the same as its object, with only the matter left aside. (This again is a position found constantly throughout the corpus in his theory of knowing, and it is not just specially devised for this occasion.) There is then no difficulty at all in the case of the immaterial, as the first being has been shown to be. The second difficulty is not dealt with directly, but we shall come back to it when discussing the next chapter, ten. The final questions in chapter nine had been touched on at the end of chapter seven, the composite in relation to the divine mind. The answer is that divine thinking does not change, and does not therefore switch from one part to another. Its object then is not composite. Human thinking about composite things takes place in a certain time, but divine thinking continues thinking itself unbroken forever.

Book Lambda ends, in chapter ten, with a consideration of how the goodness in this world is related to God. The chapter is taken up mainly with rejecting the views of other thinkers, of whom Empedocles and Anaxagoras are named, and there is clear reference to Speusippus, Plato's nephew and successor in the Academy, and reference as well to other less certainly identifiable thinkers, most probably Pythagoreans and Platonists. But the most important topic dealt with positively is this: we have seen that the world functions as it does, is as it is, because of the Supreme Being. How is the goodness in the world related to the Supreme Being? (It is assumed, following another venerable Greek tradition of thought,[7] that the world is good because of the order in the world which makes for the common good; once again, Aristotle, like Plato, does not seem to be very much concerned with the fate of individuals – they make their contribution, even if only by being dissolved (1075a23), another explanation that was to be offered time and again in the discussion of the problem of evil down through the centuries.) He answers the question of the relation of the goodness of the world to the Supreme Being once again by using an analogy. The good order in the world is obvious, just as it might be in an army. In any army it will be due to the general who is the controlling mind. It is likewise in the universe, even though the organisation varies in strictness. He uses the comparison of a large household. There it is essential that the people in charge observe a strict routine for themselves if chaos is to be avoided: one must know, for instance, where those can be found if an emergency arises or even if a change in the schedule is required. On the other hand, it is of no great importance what the occasional farmhand is doing at the particular moment or where in the yard a hen is pecking. Similarly, Aristotle seems to be arguing that the heavenly bodies are bound by strict necessity whereas human beings and others have much more freedom, simply because they are much less important – a very Platonic conception. And he ends the chapter and the book by proclaiming with Homer that there must be just one king, one ruling principle in the universe.

The mention of a Platonic conception brings us back to the beginning of this chapter. Jaeger held that Book Lambda (with the exception of chapter eight) is relatively early and still quite close to what he would call Platonism. We do not need to get involved in this debate, because there is no suggestion that Aristotle ever abandoned the views we have just outlined. It is important, however, to be aware how much reference there is in Book Lambda to the whole Greek philosophical tradition which, of course, includes Plato. This can best be achieved by considering three important and interrelated elements in Aristotle's thought: the notion of movement and self-movement, the insistence on the unchanging nature of the highest Being, and the conception of *nous*.

It might seem at first sight that Plato and Aristotle are quite close as regards their speculations about the beginning of movement. We have seen something of Plato's notion of soul as mover and self-moving motion, and we have seen that this soul is immortal. It might seem that, since Aristotle's Supreme Being is responsible for movement and is not dependent on anything else, it too might be called self-moving motion. We wish here merely to make the preliminary point that in fact Aristotle was not happy with such terminology; we shall try to explain why more fully in a moment. It hinged on his understanding of motion, *kinésis*; this to Aristotle suggested growth, alteration, local motion. Because of his theory of matter and form, potentiality and actuality, Aristotle could not remain content with the conception of a self-mover in the world. He thought, as Ross says,[8] that which moves cannot be identical with that which is moved. Plato's formulation might therefore be misleading. The mover must be transcendent. Whether the difference between himself and Plato was very great is a point we shall return to in a moment.

Plato had been impressed by Parmenides, as we saw, and his proclamation that there is no change. We have referred to his statements on the unchanging nature of the supreme reality at various places in his writings: the *Symposium, Phaedo, Republic* and *Phaedrus* come readily to mind. We have already quoted the *Statesman's* summary of what had been argued in the earlier works: 'Ever to be the same, steadfast and abiding, is the prerogative of the divinest of things only.' (269D) And yet in the dialogue which immediately preceded the Statesman there occurs the statement referred to twice already which could be taken as a challenge to Parmenides and a correction of Plato's own earlier standpoint. This is the passage in the *Sophist* (248 9) which ends: 'The philosopher must refuse to accept ... that all Reality is changeless ... He must declare that Reality or the sum of all things is both at once – all that is unchangeable and all that is in change.' (249C D) This passage is particularly interesting because of the difficulties that arise from Aristotle's retention of the notion of the immutability of the Supreme Being. There seems to be no doubt that he did retain this notion, whether we place Book Lambda early or late in his work, and in doing so he exercised a powerful influence on later thought.

We shall deal with these two questions on the moving and the unmoving in Plato and Aristotle together, but first we want to look at the third point mentioned, the continuation of the *nous* tradition. The Greek word immediately recalls Anaxagoras. It recalls also Socrates'/Plato's initial pleasure and later disappointmet at his use (Anaxogoras') of the concept, and the whole struggle to develop the notion of the immaterial in Greek thought. In Aristotle himself the passages that come to mind particularly are in the *De Anima* and the *Nicomachaean Ethics*. We find again the mixture of 'Platonism' and 'Aristotelianism' which seems to have proved so disturbing for some. *Nous* or mind is, of course, very important for Plato. Soul is the highest thing in man, and *nous* is the highest part of the soul, and through it we grasp the truth. (*Rep.* 511) The divine nature has it in its perfection, whereas man has it only to a small extent (*Tim.*51); but the human *nous* is nevertheless like the divine *nous* and is related to it (*Rep.* 611E) and is immortal with it. God sets the world in order through it (*Soph.* 265), and the *nous* which is in the world is responsible for the individual *nous* and is borne by the world soul. (*Phil.* 27C, 30C; *Tim.* 34B; *Laws* 987B)

Although we may be unwilling to identify *nous* and God in Plato, or even to talk of a transcendent *nous*, there can be no doubt that Aristotle would have found the statements from Plato just mentioned congenial. He had worked out a much more detailed theory of *nous* and the various levels of knowledge than Plato had, and this is to be seen throughout his works, from the *Analytics*, which are early, to the *Nicomachaean Ethics* and the *De Anima*, which are late. But through them all he did not depart from the doctrine which was basically Platonic: through *nous* we have true knowledge of the most perfect objects of knowledge. We are most truly mind (NE 1166al6f 22f) and it is through mind that we share in the divine nature which all things that have soul desire to share in. (*De An.* 415a29ff) Towards the end of the *Nicomachaean Ethics* he urges us to put on immortality by living the life of *nous*. 'If the mind is divine compared with man, the life of the mind must be divine compared with the life of a human creature. And we ought not to listen to those who counsel us "O man, think as man should" and "O mortal, remember your mortality". Rather ought we, so far as in us lies, to put on immortality and to leave nothing unattempted in the effort to live in conformity with the highest thing within us. Small in bulk it may be, yet in power and preciousness it transcends all the rest. We may in fact believe that this is the true self of the individual, being the sovereign and better part of him ... What is best and pleasantest for each creature is that which intimately belongs to it. So the life of the mind is the best and pleasantest for man, because the mind more than anything else is the man. Thus it will be the happiest life as well.' (1177b30ff) More 'Platonic' and less earth-bound he could hardly be, and yet this passage is taken from what some reckon to be his last work.

There is then continuity in the tradition, but it is a continuity which brought its own problems with it. We consider some of these briefly here, because although they are part of the Platonic tradition and we shall be seeing the problems raised by the history in the course of this work, nevertheless they are associated particularly with Aristotle because of his own special concepts and peculiar form of argumentation. These difficulties also go back to Parmenides, and Aristotle through his work must have shared some of the sense of triumph obvious in Plato when he saw a way around the paradoxes put forward by Parmenides and supported by Zeno. A large part of the *Physics* is taken up with such paradoxes and we have to draw on this work particularly when considering what Aristotle says about the Unmoved Mover in the *Metaphysics*.

We saw that he started his argument for the Unmoved Mover by postulating in chapter six of Book Lambda the existence of indestructible entities, based on the indestructibility of time and change. The argument is *a priori* and it depends on considerations such as those which are to be found in his discussion of the nature of the continuum in the *Physics*. It is worthwhile remarking this because, as is obvious from the *Physics*, so much of the discussion of movement had been stimulated by Parmenides' pupil, Zeno. Eristics, therefore, were in order in the debate, and one has the im-

pression that on this occasion at least Aristotle transferred unjusti-
fiably his arguments from the eristical to the metaphysical sphere.
Ross points out that the same type of argument would create the
same difficulty for Aristotle's view that space is finite.[9] St Thomas
had also pointed out that the argument is unsatisfactory in his
commentary on the *Metaphysics*: 'non enim, si ponimus tempus
quandoque incepisse, oportet ponere prius nisi quid imaginatum.'
(*In XII Met.*, lect. 5, 249 8)

A much more serious problem, however, is that which is raised
by the notion of the immutability of the Supreme Being, and since
at a later stage this notion was supported by certain texts from
scripture, it proved a lasting problem for theology.[10] The unchanging nature of the highest reality is also central to the thought
of Plato in that he insists that there must be reliability in the divine
and consistency in the human. The natural result of his establishment of the existence of unchanging moral norms and, following
on this, the existence of the unchanging Forms would be the as-
similation of all enduring things to this model. But in the later
part of his work he was gradually led to a modification of this
view. As we have seen, in the *Sophist* he will not have life and intelligence shut out from the truly real: I think we may take it that
Plato had assumed this before, but he now obviously feels that he
must be quite explicit and allow no possible doubt on the matter.
He is willing to grant that 'Reality when it is being known by the
act of knowledge must, in so far as it is known, be changed owing
to being so acted upon.' (*Soph.* 248E) He does not think that this is
a diminution of the dignity of Forms, and he is prepared to put up
with an apparent inconsistency in his own teaching for the sake of
credibility. It is clear that he is aware that the admission will
involve him in paradox, but again he is willing to accept this in
order to follow the logic of his argument. Later thinkers will not
be as ready to accept that God will be so affected by knowing.

Could we then say that, for Plato, a change from perfection to
perfection in the knowledge is a change to neither better or worse,
and this is the change in which the Supreme Mind would be involved? Perhaps not, from the dialogues, but it would not appear
to be a distortion of his thought. But when we turn back to Aristotle we find another of those apparent breaks in communication
between himself and Plato. As Skemp says, 'Aristotle seems to
leave out of account the reformation presented by the Sophists.'[11]
In Book Lambda of the *Metaphysics* Aristotle seems to think that
for the supreme *nous* to know anything other than himself would

entail reductive change. How do we account for his ignoration of the line of thought presented in the *Sophist*?

We could say simply that Aristotle did not know or did not take seriously these developments in Plato's thought. This would be a rather drastic remedy, however, and it would be better to look for something more positive. An obvious point is that we must take into account the fact that Aristotle refuses to acknowledge the existence of separate individual Forms on the Platonic model, so that there are not different perfect Forms available to the contemplation of the divine *nous*. But the explanation must be deeper. The discussion of moving in Lambda is in terms of the Greek *kinésis*. *Kinésis* in Aristotle covers the change which we know generally, including growth, alteration and locomotion. In this, some potentiality or the capacity to be brought to perfection is always involved. To rule out *kinésis* therefore for Aristotle is to rule out imperfection. He is much more rigid in his terminology than Plato, and would have been scandalised at any suggestion that in order to retain credibility we must allow *kinésis* at the highest level. But apart from terminology he is not really very far removed from Plato in his speculation about the energising which is to be found in the Highest Being. Both admit activity, and Plato indeed seems less credible than Aristotle in putting God above pleasure. Aristotle is saying that God is not bound by the conditions of the lower world because there is no imperfection in him. Therefore, he is unchanging (in the sense of *kinésis*), but because he is perfect he is always 'energising'.

This seems paradoxical to us, and the paradox is not lessened by the form which this activity takes. God's thinking is a thinking of his thinking. Does this mean that he ignores everything other than himself? One would like to believe that Aristotle does not wish it so: the last point he considers in Lambda is the relation between the world and God. Yet the way in which he expressed himself about thinking of thinking meant that the problem of God's knowledge of the world remained and many attempts to get rid of the problem have been made down through the centuries. For this reason, and many others, Book Lambda of the *Metaphysics* remained a much discussed work.

I have concentrated on Book Lambda because by general consensus it contains the bulk of Aristotle's theology while remaining firmly connected to the main body of his work. But before ending with Aristotle a couple of other theological passages should be noted. They are from the lost works, and, given the history of these fragments, we have to be even more careful with them than we are with the main body of his work. But for what it is worth we have a report that in the *De Philosophia* he argued that 'where there is a better, there is a best; among existing things one is better than another; therefore there is a best, which must be the divine.' (Fr. 1476b22 24) This is a form of argumentation that was to become popular in later Greek philosophy, and can be seen as the forerunner of St Anselm's ontological argument. More popular still, however, is the argument in the same dialogue from the existence of beauty and order in the world to the Being responsible for the design. (Fr. 1476a34ff) And finally Simplicius tells us that Aristotle held that God is either pure mind or something else beyond pure mind. (Fr. 1 Ross) This statement, too, often combined with extracts from Plato, was to have a distinguished history, particularly in Middle and Neoplatonism, which we shall be turning to after the next chapter.

CHAPTER FOUR

Hellenistic Philosophy: Stoics And Epicureans

The term Hellenistic refers to the period from the death of Alexander the Great in 323 BC to the emergence of Augustus in Rome in the first century BC. It may seem strange to consider first in this period philosophers who professed themselves to be materialists, rather than to survey the continuation of the schools of Plato and Aristotle which would seem at first sight to be a more likely source of influence on theological thinking. But, in the first place, it would be a falsification of history to suggest that there were schools more important than the Stoic and Epicurean in this period, and it would be wrong to pass over in silence their contribution to theological thinking, particularly in view of their influence on Rome and through it on the Western, Latin-speaking Church. Secondly, incongruous as it may seem to us, the materialist Stoics not only believed in God(s), but were anxious to prove the existence of God(s) and their concern for mankind. One of the great hymns to God was written by the second head of the Stoic school, Cleanthes. The Epicureans were just as anxious to show that the gods did not interfere in human affairs, and this is the driving force that gives the missionary fervour to Lucretius' faithful exposition of Epicureanism in Latin, in his great poem *On the Nature of Things*. Because of the importance of the Stoics we shall consider them before the Epicureans, even though Epicurus started teaching in Athens some six or seven years before Zeno, the first head of the Stoics, began his teaching.[1]

As might be expected, Zeno's teaching was influenced by, but was also a reaction against, that of Plato and Aristotle. Galen points up what may seem to us the incongruity of a theology among the Stoics when he contrasts Plato and Zeno talking about God: 'Plato said God was incorporeal, whereas Zeno said God was a body.' (*SVF* i 153) Not only that, but Zeno seems deliberately to have taken a position suggested by Plato in order to highlight by contrast the difference between their conceptions of reality. We have referred already to the passage in the *Sophist* where Plato advertises the necessity of introducing movement into the highest

42

level of being. In the discussion leading up to that he had debated the meaning of reality. A definition is put forward which might serve as a common ground in the debate between idealists and materialists: 'Anything has real being, that is so constituted as to possess any sort of power either to affect anything else or to be affected in however small a degree, by the most insignificant agent, though it be only once.' (247D E) The Stoics seem to have this passage in mind when they maintained that anything that was real was body. The human soul acts, therefore the human soul is a body. (*SVF* ii 790ff) They are asserting that there is no reality besides body, and they are doing so partly because their philosophic conscience would not allow them to entertain the notion of 'spirit' or *nous*, or to give it the freedom which it had been granted in Plato and Aristotle to create mystery and bafflement wherever it went.

Zeno seems to have been driven by the desire to create a consistent and testable system which would explain reality, without the need to have recourse to some mysterious spirit in any emergency which might arise. In doing so he was taking up a stance like that of his predecessors from Miletus some three hundred years before as Greek thought began to emerge from superstition. Yet he did not deny the existence of god(s) any more than they did. Zeno said that the world depended on two principles, the active and the passive, which exist together. The passive principle is matter, and the active is the *logos* in it, God. (*D.L.* vii 134) Sandbach explains this well: 'The *logos* that is God by giving shape to matter makes the world and all the things that are in it; it is rational, that is to say the world is not an arbitrary or haphazard construction; and finally the world must be seen as a dynamic process, tending to some kind of consummation, not as a static organisation with a permanent form.'[2]

Logos was a word with powerful resonance in Greek, and the fact that the Stoics put *Logos* at the centre of their world view gave their philosophy a particular importance. In classical Greek *Logos* denoted what was specifically human, reason, and that meaning is reflected in most modern European languages in words such as *logical* or words indicating various spheres of human theorising or interest, like *theology* or *archaeology*. But the word goes back well before Plato and Aristotle: Guthrie (*HGP* I pp 419 424) gives a convenient survey of its usage and meaning in earlier Greek thought. In philosophy it is notably associated with Heraclitus, a man for whom the Stoics, like Plato, had a special regard. His picture of the physical world is closely resembled by theirs. His was a world of constant change, and *panta rei*, everything is in a state of flux, could well have heen used to describe it, even if Heraclitus did not use the phrase himself. But the change was not fortuitous; it was regulated by the *Logos* which was at once the plan of things and a physical component of them. When thought of physically it was called Fire (Fr. 30) apparently to be regarded as *aither*. But it was also thought of as God, a God of many names (Fr. 67) who harmonised all the apparent discordancies in the world and so kept the world in being through life-giving tension. The man who wished to live harmoniously must also recognise this *Logos* and follow it. But the majority of men, relying on their senses alone, are so content with the superficial that they fail to see the deeper plan. (Fr. 2)

The Stoics developed the theory of Heraclitus in their own way. They said that 'in cosmic moisture God, who is the seminal principle (*spermatikos logos*) of the universe, remains behind in the moisture ... adapting matter to himself with a view to the next stage of creation.' (*D.L.* vii 136) He contains within himself the seminal principles (the *spermatikoi logoi*) in accordance with which he produces all things. (*SVF* ii 986 and 1027) Consequently, even though God is in the world and is described in material terms as fire and *pneuma* (which was credited with the special powers of both air and fire and is the binding force in the universe), God is also intelligent and artistic. The history of the word *logos* in Greek meant that when any educated person after Plato heard God described as *logos* what was suggested to him was that God was reason. Therefore the early Christians would not be as disconcerted as a normal Christian nowadays might be by a philosophy which also held that all that was real was body. The Stoics had, moreover, been engaged in a protracted debate about the distinction between man and the beasts which had been raging since at least the time of Aristotle. In that debate they maintained that it was man's possession of *logos* as manifested in his ability to communicate in meaningful language (which was also called *logos*) which marked him off from the animals. Logos in man is both internal (*endiathetos*) and expressed (*prophorikos*): it is penetrated by meaning in a way that an utterance from a parrot is not. The term which is associated with meaning in their philosophy is *lekton*, what can or is to be expressed, and the *lekton*, they said, was incorporeal. (*How* it could incorporeal the Stoics never explained).

The Stoic God, then, who is *Logos*, contains within himself the meaning of all things and gives meaning to all things. The perfect *lekton* or meaning will provide the complete truth. The Stoics described truth as the knowledge which asserts all true propositions, and this complete truth is identical with God. Human beings, as subordinate *spermatikoi logoi*, can share in the truth. It would have been tempting for a Christian philosopher to transfer this concept of God as the total truth to the Christian God, and thereby give the Christians the philosophical justification for their claim to the possession of the truth, especially in view of statements in the gospels like 'I am the way, the truth, and the life'. The popularity of *Logos* did not decrease. The *spermatikoi logoi* went easily into Latin as *rationes seminales* and expressed the Christian consciousness of God's control of the world such as we find in St Augustine. Whatever about the background and sources of St John's gospel, the Christian message could easily be represented as the perfection of this branch also of pagan philosophy, the Stoic. Christ could be presented as the *Logos* who emerges from God the Father to proclaim his truth in the world – the *logos prophorikos* expressing the *logos endiathetos*. And the *Logos* of course is also *pneuma*, Spirit. The doctrine of the Trinity could be found in Stoic philosophy. But into that I said I would not enter.

God, then, is in the world, is the world. The Stoics maintained that the world is a continuum, one, governed by the supreme *Logos*, which is also called *physis* or nature, the artistic fire going on its way to create, divine reason. Because of the Stoic insistence on unity it could be claimed by Christians later that they were actually monotheists. 'In fact, anyway, they think that God is one', as Athenagoras said. (*De Vogel* III 924b) The Stoics lent some credibility to this view by their manner of explanation of the gods of popular religion. Seneca explained that he could be called Annaeus, or Lucius, or Seneca, but the person remained the same. Similarly, God could be called by many names, but it is the same God, using his power in different ways. (*De benef.* IV 7 8) In the first line of his hymn, Cleanthes addresses Zeus as 'Most glorious of the immortals, God of many names'. De Vogel (III p.69) points out that Epictetus, a later Stoic, usually speaks of *ho theos*, God, but that on another occasion he will talk of Zeus and his government of the universe, obviously without any feeling of inconsistency.

In this the Stoics were continuing a Greek tradition which can also be traced back to Parmenides. Long reminds us that 'Parmenidean monism was taken over by Eucleides who held that "the good is one thing, called under many names" (*D.L.* ii 106)'[3] The Stoics had no wish to change this tolerant tradition; the *Logos* with them had, in many senses, become 'all in all'. But their acceptance of polytheism would make them less attractive to Christians later. What was welcome to the Christians was their series of arguments for the existence of the divine (the Christians would interpret this monotheistically, without more ado). The first of these arguements was what was later called *consensus gentium*, the 'Six million Britons cannot be wrong' argument for God's existence. This argument had a natural appeal. Besides that, Cicero tells us in two places in *On the Nature of the Gods* (ii 13 15 and iii 16), Cleanthes had four arguments to explain our belief in the gods. The first was based on the possibility of foretelling what was going to happen, the second on the benefits which men derive from the kindness of nature, the third on the terror inspired by our experience of natural phenomena and various disasters, and the fourth on the order in the universe. The 'better to best' argument which we saw in Aristotle was also employed by Cleanthes to prove the existence of God: one animal is superior to another, and man both in body and soul is better than the other animals. But man is obviously not perfect. Therefore the living being that is best would be better than man. This living being will not differ from God. Therefore God exists. (*SVF* i 529)

As Sandbach points out, this argument is fallacious, 'depending on the ambiguity of the word "best", used sometimes to mean "the best that there is", sometimes "the best that could be".'[2] But it was an extremely popular argument, as is shown by its history, and recurs in a slightly changed form in Chrysippus, the third head of the school. (*SVF* ii 1011 12) It was said, as a compliment to him, that 'If there had not been a Chrysippus, there would not have been a Stoa', and he was agreed to be a very intelligent and industrious man. But his zeal sometimes got the better of his judgement if one were to measure on the basis of arguments attributed to him of this sort: 'If there were no gods, there would be no piety. But there is piety. Therefore there are gods', or 'There are gods because there are altars'. (*SVF* ii 1017 and 1019) Chrysippus also used the argument from design (*SVF* ii 1009 10), and he was not, of course, being original in that: one has to think no further back than Plato in the *Laws*. (The Stoics were not interested in originality in these arguments, as will be obvious from what has been mentioned so far in this chapter – rather the reverse.) As we saw, Plato had to face a number of objections in his defence of the goodness of God. But Plato's difficulties could be described as negligible when compared with those faced by the Stoics. It needed all the ingenuity that Chrysippus possessed to help them weather the attacks launched on their position.

The Stoic position was particularly difficult to defend because of the nature of their materialism. They said that the world is a continuum in the process of evolution governed by a guiding plan which is immanent in the world, as a result of which everything is connected to everything else. (*SVF* ii 945) All things are linked together, and there is no such thing as chance. (*SVF* ii 967) God is responsible for the order in the universe and everything will happen according to his plan. Theoretically it is possible to explain everything by tracing the links, material naturally, between events. All man's activities, mental included, are part of this chain.

But if this is the case, is there any room for an agent other than God who can effectively determine what will happen in the world? There would not appear to be, if God is the world, the plan of the world, and the chain that determines the fate of the world. But that in turn entails difficulties. Man has the impression that he is free. Is he not really free? If he is not free, does it make any sense to talk of morality, to praise or blame him as 'good' or 'bad'? We know that men do evil things, and that there is suffering and evil in the universe. If man is not responsible, who is? Is it God?

We have been brought to this point by the mention of the argument from design. The logical development of that is the argument from God's providence. This was a topic of which the Stoics were particularly fond, in spite of the embarrassment it might bring: the second book of Cicero's *On the Nature of the Gods* gives an indication of this fondness. Chrysippus attacked Epicurus particularly for his rejection of providence: there are good gods and they look after us. (*SVF* ii 1115) The lengths to which Chrysippus went to show how the gods catered for man's needs and comforts sometimes provoked the scorn of his opponents (see De Vogel III 932); these, however, we can ignore for the moment and turn instead to the Stoic explanations of the existence of evil in a world governed by a good God.

These can be set out as follows. In the first place it can be said that from the way the wicked are punished by the gods men learn that they themselves must not act wickedly. (*SVF* ii 1175) This is an edifying explanation, of course, but apart from other weaknesses, it is of no use in explaining another part of human experience, which is that evil happens very often to the innocent and good. When confronted with this, Chrysippus apparently pondered, thinking perhaps of passages on evil from Plato and Aristotle, and replied with a question on these lines: 'Could it be that this is the sort of thing that happens in the best households, or shall we put it down to the negligence of base spirits? Or is it due to necessity, *ananke*?' (Plutarch *Stoic. Repugn.* 37) Plutarch wonders, rather acidly, whether the condemnation of Socrates, for example, is to be put on the same level as having the rubbish in the wrong place. And what sort of god would put careless, not to speak of evil, spirits in charge of the lives of human beings? Certainly not the god of Plato's *Laws*. And yet Chrysippus' third suggestion, 'necessity', is reminiscent of the *Timaeus* on the intractability of matter: God acts according to the conditions of what he finds there before him. But this sounds particularly strange in the mouth of a Stoic. Plutarch has quoted Chrysippus a little earlier (in 34) as saying: 'For no particular thing, not even the slightest, can have come about otherwise than in conformity with the universal nature and its reason (*logos*).' And Plutarch points out: 'Now, that the universal nature and the universal reason of nature are destiny and providence and Zeus, of this not even the Antipodes are unaware'.

The Stoics, then, since it seemed unfitting to attribute negligence or incompetence or ill-will to God, were forced to put forward arguments on the lines of 'you can't make an omelette without breaking eggs'. Some bad things happen not because they are directly willed, but because they are a necessary accompaniment of 'natural' processes: they come *kata parakolouthésin*. That is the explanation of diseases, according to Chrysippus. The very delicacy of the construction of human beings, for instance, leaves them liable to diseases and accidents which cruder structures do not experience – the human head is a good example (*SVF* ii 1170). This argument has a certain attractiveness, as has its extension: Chrysippus admits that good people do sometimes suffer, but that evil of this sort is not aimed at them directly. An arrangement which is for the good of the city as a whole may impinge on an individual. (*SVF* ii 1176) We may think of a ring road which spares the centre of the city long-distance traffic but happens to be built alongside your once quiet house in the suburbs.

Psychologically these arguments are more satisfying than the logical one (which recalls Heraclitus) that contraries are connected and that you cannot have one without the other. Justice implies injustice, bravery, cowardice, and likewise good implies evil. Chrysippus calls on Plato to support him in this (apparently *Phaedo* 60B C is meant), but does not refer to Aristotle, *Cat.* 10, where he points out that not all opposites are of this sort, among them the good and bad. (See De Vogel III pp 80 81)

The Stoics had one final argument which found favour with Christians later. They maintained that God tried the best people with suffering, just as in the army the most dangerous tasks are assigned to the best soldiers. Good people then should accept suffering as a mark of honour, and say 'God has judged us the right people on whom to measure how much human nature can endure'. (Seneca *On Providence* IV)

Another possible explanation of evil is of course to say that it is due to man who is left free by God, and as a result will have either merit or demerit. The difficulty about this argument for the Stoics is that it is hard to see how man can really be called free, as we saw. Chrysippus attempts to avoid complete determinism, using the analogy of the cylinder and introducing a distinction between perfect and principal causes on the one hand and auxiliary and proximate on the other. (*SVF* ii 974) The cylinder will *roll* if pushed, but the fact that it will roll when pushed is attributable to itself. Its *volubilitas*, 'rollableness' Chrysippus calls the principal and perfect cause of its movement, while the push is the auxiliary and proximate cause. But the perfect and principal cause of the subsequent action is the assent which is within our power. And so apparently our freedom, and the possibility of calling our actions good or bad, are preserved.

Without going as far as Plutarch and saying that this line of reasoning is 'in violent contradiction to the doctrine of destiny', (*Stoic. Repugn.* 47) we may say that the Stoics have left questions unanswered. But in this they are not unique, and later attempts to reconcile the existence of evil and the existence of an all-powerful, benevolent (though, in later cases, spiritual) God, have not been noticeably more successful. That the Stoics attempted and failed to give a coherent answer to the problem of evil is not to be wondered at. More remarkable and worth pondering, in view of the motive postulated for their materialism, the reaction against the 'spiritualism' of Plato and Aristotle, is the fact that in order to theorise at all, they had to introduce entities which they called incorporeals into their system. Among these would be ranked 'meanings'. Aristotle would have found it piquant that the 'meaning' of the Stoic universe would have to be found outside it, since it was not a body, and nothing exists but bodies.

We need not devote much space to the Epicureans as thinkers about theology, for though they believed that gods existed, they did not believe that they concerned themselves with the world, and therefore considered it foolish to try to make them interfere in the world by prayers and sacrifices and what they regarded as other forms of superstition. We have surmised that the Stoics developed their materialistic system because of their unwillingness to accept a world where 'spirit' was as important as it is in the systems of Plato and Aristotle. In the case of the Epicureans we do not have o depend on surmise. While we still have to rely to a large extent on fragments for our knowledge of Epicurus' teaching, we have at least some longer pieces of continuous exposition from his own pen, and we also have the long poem in Latin by Lucretius which is, as far as we can check it, remarkably faithful to the teachings of his master.

Lucretius, particularly, makes it clear that the Epicurean system was developed to free men from the fears that belief in the existence of spirit gives rise to. For if the soul survives as spirit there is the possibility that the stories, told by Plato among others, of punishments in another world after death may be true. Therefore, Epicurus insists, there is no afterlife: the soul, like the body, is made up of atoms, and when death occurs, the soul-atoms are scattered just as the body decays. No 'personality', disembodied, survives. There is nothing but body: the universe consists of atoms and the void.

But if there is no afterlife, how do we explain the widespread fear of death, of suffering in an afterlife, 'that fear of Acheron ... which troubles the life of man from its deepest depths, suffuses all with the blackness of death, and leaves no delight clean and pure'? (Lucretius *DRN* 3, 37 40) Lucretius, following Epicurus we presume, explains that all these stories of sufferings in an afterlife are really projections of our fears in this life: mythology about the afterlife is misunderstood psychology. So, for example, the story of Tantalus represents the paralysis of men in the face of superstition, Tityos the effects of passion, Sisyphus the results of ambition. These are all stories to illustrate the power of the guilty conscience fearing retribution at any moment, which is whipped, gnawed and burnt through its own fault and its own lack of philosophy. 'The fool's life at length becomes a hell on earth.' (*DRN* 3, 1023) This psychological explanation of the afterlife was to have a great future, and humane Christians would use it to avoid the embarrassment of a crude physical picture of the punishments of hell. But they would not accept with it the Epicurean explanation of death as simply the scattering of atoms of body and soul once more amidst the void.

The gods exist and are also constituted from atoms. We can be certain that they do exist because of the universal belief in their existence and because in dreams we have visions of gods where they appear in human form. But they have not made our world and do not interfere with it. That the world is not the handiwork of the gods is obvious: the faults in it are too great (Lucretius 5,

156 194). The world has been formed by the collision of the atoms: there followed on this the separation out of the elements and then a gradual evolution of the various species. By such a process the human race developed. We know that the gods exist in spite of their non-interference and people have seen them because the film-image that constantly comes out from them penetrates to the fine mind-atoms without the intervention of the senses. They exist in the spaces between the worlds, resting eternally (Lucretius 3, 18 24), and communicating with each other in a language something like Greek. (Philodemus, *De Dis* 3, col. 13 and 14, pp 36 7 Diels) In that happy condition we may leave them.

CHAPTER FIVE

The Schools of Plato and Aristotle

The very title of this chapter indicates that we may not expect much originality from the successors of the two great masters up until the third century AD. The name Neoplatonism, given to the philosophy of Plotinus more than five hundred years after the death of Plato, is a further indication that, at least in the eyes of moderns, nothing outstanding was produced by the thinkers in between. But so much has been lost that such a judgement may be not only harsh but hazardous. It is generally agreed that it was an age of 'scholasticism' where more value was placed on preserving and passing on in summary fashion a fairly fixed range of answers to what were regarded as the most important philosophical questions. Among these was the question of God. This is particularly obvious in the second half of this period. As Dillon says, 'throughout our period, the question of the nature and activity of the supreme principle, or God, is dominant'.[1] The period was, then, even if not original, nevertheless an important one in the establishment of set ways of talking about God. It was also a period during which the most important 'theologies', Platonic, Aristotelian and Stoic, were brought together and made serviceable for the co-ordinating genius of Plotinus. From there particularly they passed on to the Christian world.

We begin by looking briefly at the immediate successors of Plato, Speusippus and Xenocrates, not just for the sake of tidiness, but because it appears, as far as we can see, that they were largely responsible for what was later accepted as typical Platonism. I said, 'as far as we can see', because we are in no better position as regards the knowledge of the thought of these men than we were in regard to Zeno, the first Stoic. The fragments preserved are wretchedly meagre, and, of course, as is frequently the case, not always preserved by friends. But we may deduce from them the following concerning Speusippus, the nephew of Plato, and his successor as head of the Academy.

Aristotle said that Speusippus' version of reality was like a badly constructed tragedy, one thing following on another with no necessary connection between them. We do not have enough of Speusippus' teaching to be quite sure what Aristotle was being critical of, and Aristotle may also have had other reasons for being unkind to Speusippus, but it has been suggested that Aristotle's criticism certainly included a feature which is of interest for later theological speculation. According to Aristotle (*Met.* 1092all 15) in the system of Speusippus 'The One itself is not even being'. We learn from a fragment of Speusippus preserved in *Iamblichus* that the One is superior to Being because of its simplicity and because it is the principle of everything else. We cannot even talk of the One as beautiful or good because it is superior to these and the cause of them.[2] We do not need to deal at any more length with the system of Speusippus, and we cannot be certain of the extent of his influence on later Platonism. But this insistence on the utter transcendence of the One, together with Plato's God 'beyond Being', is a note that will be heard again and again with reference to God in the succeeding centuries until the climax in Plotinus. As Dodds says: 'It seems to me that with Speusippus we are already well started on the road to Neoplatonism'. (art. cit. 140)

Speusippus was followed by Xenocrates as head of the Academy. Guthrie says that he 'tended to see everything in theological terms'.[3] In this he is typical of the period with which we shall be concerned in this chapter. The most remarkable feature in his thought to our eyes in his interest in 'daemons'. These are to be thought of, like the personified Eros in the *Symposium*, as spirits intermediary between God and man. They assumed more and more importance with the increasing emphasis on the utter transcendence of God: God could not be defiled with contact with the lowest levels of creation, and man's desire to make contact could be realised only through intermediaries. So, as Merlan says, 'From the time of Xenocrates on, the belief in good and evil spirits became universal in Platonism'.[4]

Not only there was Xenocrates influential. Dillon speaks of him as 'a man who may indeed be termed the second founder of Platonism.[5] The urge to systematise the thoughts which Plato deliberately left fluid is obvious in him. In this he resembles Aristotle, his contemporary, and sets a precedent for those Platonists who followed him, and looked up to him. A tidy, coherent system was much in demand, and this was provided by Xenocrates. He is reported (frr. 15,16) to have held that the supreme principles are the Monad and the Dyad. The Monad is the male principle, with the place of father in the universe, and he is the first God, who is also *nous*, intellect or mind.

There is nothing new, as we have seen, in calling God mind. The notion did not originate with Aristotle, and in view of the tradition it is unlikely that the Platonist even of the strictest persuasion would feel inhibited from calling his God Mind simply because this notion is so prominent in Book Lambda. What is more disputable, however, is the extent to which Platonists would actually be influenced by Aristotelian speculation. I am inclined to the view that, just as Aristotle remained in many ways always a Platonist, so too the mutual influence of the two schools must never be underestimated. All this by way of introduction to the next interesting question which is raised in the discussion of Xenocrates. This is the question of the Forms or Ideas as the thoughts of God.[6]

Plato had not only allowed but encouraged disagreement with the theories which he put forward in the Academy: an example of such encouragement is the first half of the *Parmenides* on the existence and nature of the Forms. He could not, then, have been surprised that not one of his most distinguished pupils, neither Speusippus, Xenocrates, nor Aristotle, remained 'faithful' to his theory of Forms. In the case of Xenocrates we are told that he replaced the Forms in his system of the universe with numbers, so that the highest places in his structure would be occupied by the First Principles, the Monad and the Dyad, followed by the numbers in second place. Now, if Xenocrates' universe was unified, as it apparently was, there would be contact between the first and second levels, and what more natural contact could there be than that of the numbers in the Mind of the One. It has, therefore, been suggested[7] that it is Xenocrates who is ultimately responsible for the notion of the Forms as the Thoughts of God, a theory designed to allow God to have contact with the world without being sullied by it. This notion certainly has a powerful influence in later Platonism, and we shall consider it more fully in that context. It has been mentioned here merely to indicate that Platonism might have been joined with Aristotelianism even at an early stage to produce a theory which could be held by both.

So much for the immediate successors of Plato. Aristotle's successor, Theophrastus, is himself proof that relations were not necessarily bad between the schools. Xenocrates is given credit by Theophrastus in his *Metaphysics* (6b7ff) for his thoroughness in working out the details of his universe. On the other hand, Theophrastus makes some perceptive criticisms of his friend and master Aristotle's ruling principle, while agreeing with him on the overall position. For instance, he agrees with Aristotle that 'the

universe is not a mere series of episodes' (4al4); and that 'the ruling principle of all things, through which all things both are and
endure, is divine'.(4bl5f) He agrees also that the ruling principle is
the cause of movement, is itself unmoved, and is the object of desire because of which there is continuous and unceasing circular
motion. (4b21ff) But he finds it strange that the one mover does
not move all bodies with the same motion, and furthermore it is
not at all clear how harmony is preserved. Above all, it is hard to
see why desire for the Unmoved produces not rest but motion;
the former would be the more fitting in this case. (5al7ff) He repeats this point at 7b23ff, and it obviously bothered him.

His most interesting objection to Aristotle, however, is that
concerning his theology. This is important to the philosophy of
religion because of the popularity which the argument for God's
existence from design in the world has always enjoyed and for the
notion of God's providence which is closely connected with it. A
constant refrain in Aristotle is that God and nature do nothing in
vain. Theophrastus was well aware of this attitude of Aristotle's.
But he points out modestly: 'With regard to the view that all things
are for the sake of an end and nothing is in vain, the assignation of
ends is in general not easy (where should we begin and with what
sort of things should we finish?), and in particular some things
are difficult because they do not seem to be for the sake of an end
but to occur, some of them, by coincidence, and others, by some
necessity'. (l0a22ff) What is the purpose of the tides, for instance,
or breasts in males, or beards in some animals? After these and
similar questions, he asserts: 'We must set certain limits to pur-
posiveness and to the effort after the best, and not assert it to exist
in all cases without qualification'. (llalff) Exaggerated statements
only give rise to scepticism, as, for instance, when we are told that
'where the better is possible, there it is never lacking' (lla8f),
which seems to be another allusion to the argument later to be
known as the ontological, which we have seen in Aristotle and the
Stoics.

These are eminently sensible observations by Theophrastus.
The Stoics would have saved themselves much trouble if they had
received his warning about excessive zeal in arguments from design. We would all have been spared much nonsense down the
centuries if his specific questions had been heeded. But in fact the
fragment now called Theophrastus' *Metaphysics* seems to have
disappeared during the heyday of Stoicism and to have remained
unnoticed until the first century BC. Even if it had attained more
prominence, of course, it is quite likely that it would have been re-

jected by pious Stoics as the work of an atheist. Theophrastus
however was not an atheist: Professor De Vogel writes, 'He considered atheism as an abnormality and a great sin'. (II p 237)
Equally quaintly, Merlan says, 'There is particularly no trace that
he ever envisioned first philosophy to be anything but theology.'[8]
He wrote a work on piety and regarded belief in the gods as the
natural state. But it could be maintained that Theophrastus
marked the beginning of a naturalistic movement in the school of
Aristotle which led in the end to its disappearance as an identifiable group. Theophrastus' successor, Strato, was marked even by
his soubriquet, the *Physikos*, as a continuer of the naturalistic
movement. Those in the school who were primarily interested in
the question of God or the gods were more and more absorbed
into Platonism. And it is back to Platonism that we now must turn
to see the continuation of the history of philosophy as theology.

Xenocrates died in 314 BC, and the headship of the Academy
then passed into the hands of men who did not contribute anything that we need concern ourselves with. The most interesting
development in the Academy in the century after Plato's death
was the turn towards scepticism and the notion of the withhold-
ing of assent under Arcesilaus. The greatest of his successors in
this tradition was Carneades, who employed his wits against
many Stoic positions, including their polytheism. But we have to
pass over this entertaining character and turn to the ensuing dogmatic phase in the Academy, from the first century BC to the third
AD, which is conveniently called Middle Platonism.

It would be tedious to sift the writings of each of these philosophers for the theological grains which might emerge. It would
also be misleading to give the impression that they form a tightly
knit group with a fixed body of doctrine around which lay exterior
darkness. Nevertheless, some ideas keep recurring so frequently
that they are hallmarks of Middle Platonism. Some of these have
already been mentioned and I shall now add others. We have
seen, for instance, the emphasis on the absolute transcendence of
God. This insistence led eventually to the so-called negative theology. But the way of negation was only one of the ways to God
which was discovered to have existed in Plato's work. And contact with God was also sought not only through the 'daemons', already mentioned, but also through what was called the Second,
and sometimes the Third, God, who took various forms. He might
be called the *Logos*, Reason or the *nous*, mind, of God. God's contact with the world was assured in turn by the fact that he had the
exemplars, or Forms, of the world in his Mind. The creation of the
world was also a much canvassed topic and gave scope for the ac-

tivity of the Second and Third God or other beings, at this or a slightly lower level. The world as created was generally assumed to be controlled by the good principle, but the existence of evil was also accepted and the independent existence of an evil principle was also occasionally admitted. Turning towards the good principle and so becoming like to God was generally accepted as the purpose of life. Even those who insisted on the independent existence of an evil principle believed that God's providence was active in the world and that man was free to do good or evil under this providence. The Stoics certainly did their share to make this an important issue. For, finally, we should remember that, while we may class these thinkers as Middle Platonists, various traditions were drawn on and used when convenience or the logic of the argument demanded it – Pythagoreans, Peripatetics and Stoics. Such alliances seemed preferable to defeat at the hands of the Sceptics. The lead in this direction had been given by Antiochus of Ascalon (c. 130 68 BC).[9]

We may consider first the notion of the transcendence of God. The Middle Platonists were naturally always glad to be able to claim Plato as an authority for a position and a number of favourite passages were frequently invoked. The 'beyond Being' in the Republic seemed to give ample justification in regard to transcendence. The *Parmenides*, with its discussion of the One which, if it exists, cannot be named or known, could also be utilised, as could passages in the *Sophist* and *Philebus*. The Second Letter (312E) might indicate the existence of intermediate gods. Finally, the Seventh Letter, with its insistence on the impossibility of communicating the highest truth, could easily fit in with the general conviction of the hidden nature of God. Speusippus' position would, apparently, help to confirm this attitude: another authority was always welcome to middle Platonists.

In the nature of the case, it is impossible to declare firmly that Middle Platonism began in such and such a year with such and such a person. But Eudorus of Alexandria in the middle of the first century BC is probably as good a candidate as any for the title of founder. In his case too we have to rely on later reports of his teaching, but if we can depend on these and take into account the habit of using 'authorities' to cover one's own views, we may postulate that Eudorus believed that at the highest level there existed the supreme One, with another One on the level beneath the highest. The supreme One be called the *hyperanó theos*, the God above. A much better known Alexandrian, Philo (c 20 BC - after 40 AD) leaves no doubts at all about his views on the transcendental God.

Philo, of course, is not a typical case, for he is an Alexandrian Jew, and is drawing on the Old Testament almost in a spirit of competition with Greek philosophy. But there is no mistaking his devotion to Plato as well as to Moses, and his language about God reflects not only the Septuagint, but also the Academy. So God is the One, the Monad, but also beyond the One and the Monad. He is ineffable, beyond human language, he cannot be named and he cannot be grasped. He transcends the Good Itself and the Beautiful Itself.

There is no disputing Philo's influence on Christian thinkers like the Alexandrian theologians, even if one is unwilling to grant him much on Middle Platonism in general. Whatever about his influence, his language about God's transcendence is certainly typical of Middle Platonism. Middle Platonism was by this time very much open to Pythagoreanism, and in Moderatus (c 1 AD - 70 AD) we have a figure who is believed to have anticipated the system of Plotinus, not least in his postulation of a First One, God, above all being. Plutarch (c 45AD - 120AD) is the next considerable Platonist we know of and God's transcendence is central to his thought. Only God truly is and he alone is truly one (*De E* 391-393), utterly removed from all that is subject to destruction and death. The same emphasis on the remoteness of God, the ineffable, unnameable, immeasurable is to be found in Apuleius (b c 123 AD), and about the same time in the Neopythagorean-Platonist Numenius. His first God is at rest, removed from all activity and creations which is left to his son, the second God (Frr. 12 and 15). He describes vividly (Fr. 2) how we must strive to catch a glimpse of this God, the Good, like someone trying from a lookout post to spy a small boat in a high sea. It is interesting also that Numenius speaks with great respect of the God of the Jews. (Fr. 56)

Numenius had a powerful influence on succeeding Platonists, and especially on the greatest of all, Plotinus. But for us the most revealing work of all this period is that of Albinus, a slightly older contemporary of Apuleius and Numenius. We have from him a short *Introduction to Plato* and a longer and very influential work, the *Didaskalikos* which is a summary of the accepted Platonism of the time. It is all the more important because it apparently makes no claim to originality, but sets out in textbook fashion the central Platonic doctrines. Chapter Ten is devoted to God. We are told that God is eternal, ineffable, perfectly self-sufficient (*autotelés*), eternally perfect (*aeitelés*), and entirely perfect (*pantelés*). The problem then arises, how can imperfect man make contact with such perfection? Albinus shows that there are three ways, and it is obvious that here again he is not innovating. The first way is that 'by removal', what was later called the way of negation: we come to the notion of a point by removing gradually the parts of a body, taking the line as one aspect of the surface and then removing the line. The second way is that of analogy, and here again the best example is that of Plato's *Republic*: as the sun is to the objects of vision, so the first mind is to the world of spirit. The third way is equally clearly based on the *Symposium* of Plato, and is the way of ascent (or the *via eminentiae* as it was later called): we move gradually upwards from the lesser beauties to the perfection of beauty, the final object of desire.

It seems obvious that Albinus is not innovating here, partly because of the matter of fact manner in which the three ways are introduced, but also because of the occurrence of essentially the same scheme in a work roughly contemporary with that of Albinus, the *Alethes Logos* of Celsus. Origen tells us that Celsus quoted the *Timaeus* on the difficulty of coming to God, and said that for that reason the following three ways had been thought out, 1) that of composition, which corresponds to that of ascent, 2) that of analysis, which seems to be that of negation, and 3) that which Census also calls analogy. (*Contra Celsum* vii 42) Both authors seem to regard the ways as well established methods of making contact with the God whose transcendence is obviously a favourite theme of the age.

The development of the three ways is one indication of the awareness that insistence on the transcendence of God might lead to a situation where God is thought of as utterly remote from the world in the bad sense of not caring what happened in the world. The Epicureans were called atheists on account of this attitude. It is an attitude which, as we saw, has also been attributed to Aristotle. Among the Middle Platonists we find a strong attack on Aristotle by Plutarch, for instance: 'The true God has a beautiful and fitting variety of spectacles in numerous worlds to look at. He does not look at an empty infinity outside himself and does not concentrate his attention on himself and nothing else, as some people have imagined.' (*De def. orac.* 426D) Aristotle is not mentioned, but the reference to the *Eudemian Ethics* 1245b14 seems unmistakable. Atticus, 'a philosopher of the Platonic school', writing at least half a century after Plutarch, perhaps about 180 AD, is much more severe on Aristotle and mentions him by name. Aristotle attributes to the gods the same insouciance about the world as does Epicurus; Aristotle in fact is even worse than Epicurus. (Fr. 3, Baudry)

But it cannot be said that this was the typical attitude to Aristotle's Unmoved Mover throughout this period. It was common to take a much more positive approach to Aristotle's God, and indeed, as Dillon says, from the time of Xenocrates, 'the essentially Aristotelian concept of a self-contemplating divine mind is that which is dominant in all subsequent official Platonism up to Plotinus'.[10] The divine mind was brought into contact with the world by a happy mixture of doctrines from Platonism, Aristotelianism and Stoicism. One form of this blending was the notion that the Forms or Ideas are the thoughts of God and are to be found in his mind. We have seen that it has been suggested that Xenocrates, the third head of the Academy, may already have taken the decisive step in this direction. Plato himself had specifically rejected the notion that the Forms were thoughts in the *Parmenides*, but as we also saw he did not insist on a party line in these matters, and, according to Diogenes Laertius (iii 13), Alcimus, who was roughly a contemporary of Plato, held that the Forms are in the soul. There has been much dispute as to whether the notion was first given canonical form by Antiochus, Posidonius or Arius Didymus, but for our purposes it is sufficient to note that it appears without claims for originality in Philo, and from then on it is a recurring feature. We find it in Seneca (Ep. 45), in Nicomachus (c 100AD – 150), and we have an interesting treatment in Albinius or Alcinous. In chapter nine of the *Didaskalikos* he begins his definition of the idea by saying, 'The Form is, considered in relation to God, his thought'. A little later he sets out to prove that the Forms or Ideas must exist, and his first argument is: whether God is Mind, or a being with mind, in either case he must have thoughts (*noémata*), and these must be eternal and unchanging; if this is so, the Forms exist'. The discussion of the Forms and their association with God is carried over into chapter ten. The First God is the Mind which moves the mind of the whole heaven. As the object of desire it sets desire in motion, while remaining itself motionless. Alcinous continues, 'Since the first Mind is the noblest of things, the object of its thought must also be noblest, and nothing is nobler than it is itself; so therefore it would have to contemplate eternally itself and its own thoughts'.

It is obvious that Alcinous has here, unabashed, transplanted Aristotle's God of Book Lambda into the centre of Platonism. But it would have seemed to him a quite logical procedure: Plato's Forms were the object of longing and *a fortiori* his God must be the object of desire. Plutarch would not have disagreed with this (see *De Fac.* 944E) he simply wanted more emphasis on God's providence than Alcinous seemed to be concerned for. Middle Platonism in general, through its tolerance of the doctrines of other schools, was able to leave room for God's providence to its own satisfaction. Once again we can observe the process in Philo: 'As then the city which was fashioned beforehand within the mind of the architect held no place in the outer world, but had been imprinted on the soul of the craftsman as by a seal, even so the world that consists of the Forms would have no other location than the divine Reason (*logos*), which was the author of this physical world.' (*Opif.* 20) Philo calls the *logos* the Son, the Second God.[11] The *Logos* is the image of God, and all Forms are contained in it.

Logos is a respectable Platonic word, and the concept plays an important role in Plato's thought. But there is no mistaking the Stoic influence on the concept in Philo. (This is not to say that Philo was original here either: Antiochus may well have taken the first step.) The Stoic *logos prophorikos* can be interpreted as God's expression of himself in the world. The *logos spermatikos* is the overall seminal principle or reason which rules the world and sees that the world plan is unfolded through the subordinate *logoi spermatikoi* or seminal principles which it contains. By making these equivalent to the Platonic Forms and making them reside in the *Logos*, which in turn is made equivalent to the *Demiourgos* or Maker of the *Timaeus*, Philo managed to combine God's providence with his transcendence, because the First God is still unsullied with creation. In this path he was followed by others. The passage just quoted from Philo (*Opif.* 20) is echoed in Plutarch (*De Is.* 373AB) where the images of the Good and Intelligible and Real appear in the world, and the *logoi* are like figures stamped on wax. The Forms or *Logos* which appear in matter are dependent on the transcendent God. Plutarch is not necessarily imitating Philo: the manner of thought is simply congenial to both. How easy it was to combine what could be Stoicism with Platonism and Aristotelianism can be seen from a passage in Plutarch's *De Sera* (550Df). The latter half of the passage is an obvious reference to the *Timaeus*. The intervention of the *Demiourgos*, Maker or Craftsman, meant that the soul came to try to share in the form and excellence of God. The sight of the beauty and order of the heavenly bodies encourages man to cultivate beauty and order within himself. For his purpose in life is to become like unto God.

We have referred above to Atticus' attack on Aristotle because of the uncaring attitude of Aristotle's God. (Fr. 3) In one of his frequent recurrences to this favourite theme, he points out that everything happens according to providence in Plato, whereas

Aristotle disagrees with all this. (Fr.8, Baudry) He supports this contention in language which can only be called Platonised Stoicism. For, according to Atticus, Plato says that the soul sets the universe in order, going through all of it. Nature is nothing else but soul, and clearly not irrational soul (*alogos*). It binds all things together. We are again being presented with the Stoic *logos* but now in Platonic dress.

Finally, if we may turn back to Alcinous again as the Middle Platonist textbook, we can see how the mingling of traditions enables him to preserve the transcendence of God and yet make sure that the world is providentially ordered through this God. He tells us later on in chapter ten that God is called father 'because he, as the cause of all things, sets in order the heavenly Mind and the soul of the world in accordance with himself and his thoughts. By his own will he has filled all things with himself, as being the cause of its Mind. And this, being set in order by the Father, itself sets in order the whole of Nature within this world'. We can see in this, I think, at least three levels: the First God, then secondly, the Mind of the world which is enlivened by God, but which is active in the third, that is, the Soul of the World, so guaranteeing proper order.

Because of the desire to combine transcendence and providence, this scheme of a First God, and then a second-level being, who or which communicates with a third level, is another recurrent feature in Middle Platonism. We saw the beginnings of such a scheme in Speusippus and Xenocrates. Eudorus had his supreme One above the principles of the Monad and the Dyad which are active in the universe. Philo has his own special reasons for insisting on the one supreme God, but with the help of Stoicism brings in the *Logos*, like the *Demiourgos*, to be the intermediary with the world. Plutarch too talks of the Supreme God and the intermediary *Logos*. Moderatus has his First One, but also a system of Three Ones. Numenius, Proclus tells us, 'proclaims three gods, calling the first "Father", the second "Creator", and the third "Creation". (Fr. 21) Apuleius too talks of the First God, where the second seems to be *nous* or *Logos*.

This development cannot be claimed to be due to any emergent Christian Trinitarian thinking. It is simply an endeavour to preserve contact between God and the world. It was the same endeavour which produced the crop of daemons that are also a feature of this period. Xenocrates is commonly given the credit or discredit for stimulating this development, but it is obvious that it could be derived from a literal-minded approach to Plato's dialogues. The occurrence of daemons in Philo, for instance, is due as much to Plato as to the Old Testament, and in fact he settles difficulties in Genesis by appeal to the *Timaeus*. (see *Opif*. 72ff) The *Symposium* and the *Phaedrus* (247A) prove the existence of good daemons (*Gig*. 12; *Sacr*. 5), and the *Laws* may have helped him to develop his equally firm conviction of the existence of evil daemons. (*Somn*. 1 17-18)

Plutarch was a great admirer of Xenocrates and cites him for what might be called the scientific theory of daemons. In Academic fashion, Xenocrates had apparently worked out a method of application of triangles to the universe, and the daemons were fitted into this. There are daemons of various sorts. God has appointed some as his servants to punish us, but some other daemons are by nature, so to speak, nasty and bad and need to be treated with respect. Some daemons of this kind unfortunately take an individual interest in us. (*Tranquillity of Mind* 474B) We are lucky enough, in view of the existence of such devils, to have the support of guardian daemons who will help us out when things get really difficult. (*On the Daemon of Socrates* 593Dff)

Plutarch was the most important continuer of the tradition of demonology in middle Platonism, which is to be found again in Albinus, but the fullest account is to be found in Apuleius, in *De Deo Socratis*, starting again from the basic principle that since there must be contact between God and man, there must be intermediaries and these are daemons. It would be tedious to go through his account of the various types which, in any case, differs little from that of Plutarch. It is more rewarding to turn to a question which the very mention of 'demon' raises for modern readers. That is, by what authority do the evil daemons operate, what is their basis, what is their domain? In other words, is there an independent evil principle in the world which is the explanation of the existence of evil?

We saw that Plato's language in some of the dialogues left him open to the accusation that he was a dualist. Whether or not this was true, there is a tradition of dualism to be found in Middle Platonism, and it is interesting in view of his demonology that Plutarch is one of the representatives of it. The possibility of such a development was inherent in Plato's exaltation of the spiritual above the corporeal in general, apart altogether from passages like those in the *Statesman, Timaeus* and *Laws*. Matter was talked of as a source of contamination. In the later Academic tradition, a principle representing matter was to be found, which was frequently called the Dyad and which was set over against the One or the Monad which represents Form. In many Platonists, the One or supreme One or Monad is unquestionably the dominant directing principle which merely uses matter. But it is the other Platonists in whom we are interested and the first of these is Plutarch. He refers to the *Laws* specifically as an authority for his view. Plato's opinion on the question might have been obscure in earlier dialogues, but, he says, 'in the *Laws*, when he had grown considerably older, he asserts, not in circumlocution or symbolically, but in specific words, that the movement of the universe is actuated not by one soul, but perhaps by several, and certainly by not less than two, and of these the one is beneficent, and the other is opposed to it, and the artificer of things opposed'. (*De Is.* 370F) He rejects Monism such as that of the Stoics (369A), and calls on even older authorities than Plato for his dualism. It is, indeed, 'the laws of Nature that nothing comes into being without a cause, and if the good cannot provide a cause for evil, then it follows that Nature must have in herself the source and origin of evil, just as she contains the source and origin of good. The great majority and the wisest of men hold this opinion: they believe that there are two gods, rivals as it were, the one the Artificer of good and the other of evil. There are also those who call the better one a god and the other a daemon, as, for example, Zoroaster the Sage, who, they record, lived five thousand years before the time of the Trojan War'. (Ibid 369E)

Whatever about Plutarch's chronology, there is no doubting his conviction about dualism. The problem of evil is one of the three great problems which were later to haunt the young Augustine. He found his solution through the reading of the Neoplatonists. Plotinus was to reject dualism, as indeed were most of the Platonists between Plutarch and himself. But one of the most interesting of these, Numenius, agreed with Plutarch. Plutarch had referred to the Pythagorean opposites also among his authorities. (ibid 370E) Numenius stood very much in the Pythagorean tradition. Like Plutarch, he can call on *Laws* to back his dualist position. The Dyad, he says, is opposed to the Monad, and Matter, of which the Dyad is the principle, is not just neutral but positively evil. The *Demiourgos* in the *Timaeus*, as he points out, has to contend with something which he can never entirely abolish. And so, according to Numenius 'there cannot be found in the realm of generation any entity free from vice'. This applies of course to individuals: Numenius is extremely Platonic in his insistence that it is for the soul a fall to come into the body, and he even outdoes Plato in his presentation of the tragedy it is for the soul to be associated with the body. (Frr. 30-35,48)

It would appear that dualism of this sort must inevitably have repercussions for another topic much debated in Middle Platonism, the question of whether or not the world has come into being in time. We do not find this question discussed in the fragments of Numenius that are preserved, but Proclus links it with the two other dualists in the tradition, Plutarch and Atticus. (Atticus, like Plutarch, according to Proclus, grasped eagerly at *Timaeus* 30A to support his belief in an evil soul which pre-existed creation and was responsible for disorderly motion.) Once again, the question has a long history. From the very beginning there had been interpretations of Plato's creation doctrine in the *Timaeus*. His immediate successors, Speusippus and Xenocrates, held that Plato merely talked in terms of time because this was unavoidable but that really creation was eternal and should not be thought of in terms of time. Aristotle, on the other hand, blames Plato for suggesting that the world had a beginning in time. (*De Caelo* I 12; II 2) Crantor shortly afterwards said that 'created' meant 'dependent on a cause other than itself'. (Proclus *In Tim* I 277,8) Plutarch tells us that Eudorus held the same view as Xenocrates and Crantor. (*Proc. An.* 1013B) Philo wrote a special treatise called *On the Creation of the World*. He, too, holds that there is not creation in time, but creation in the sense that the world depends for its existence on God. Whether Philo also believed that God created matter as well and so believed in creation *ex nihilo* is more doubtful. Calvenus Taurus, whose dates are about 100-165 AD, apparently admired Plutarch but did not agree with him about creation in time. We have quite an elaborate discussion of the meanings of the word *genetos*, 'created', preserved from his *Commentary on the Timaeus* (See Dillon, 1977, 242-4). Though we cannot be absolutely certain, Calvenus appeared to favour the meaning of 'created' as depending on an outside source which is responsible for order. Alcinous is quite explicit: 'When Plato says the world is "created", we must not understand this to mean that there was ever a time when there was no world; what it means is that it is constantly in a state of coming-to-be, and reveals a cause of its existence more sovereign than itself'. (*Did* c 14)

Platonists in general, whatever their differences about creation in time, might be expected to be believers in providence, and we have seen that in fact they were. But a 'strong' belief in providence brings with it, as we saw in the case of the Stoics, the difficulty of allowing for free will in man, and of accounting for the apparently fated evils that befall particularly the good man. We have now to consider the Middle Platonist response to this problem. We have to remember that the fact that the Stoics were themselves such great defenders of providence had its influence on Middle Platonism which, as we have seen already, was tolerant of views of whatever origin which helped to ccnfirm their own position. But the Stoic defence had raised sceptical objections and these too were inherited by Middle Platonism. Moreover, the Platonists themselves were wary of excessive Stoic emphasis on fate.

We may begin our survey with a glance at Philo, since there is some doubt about whether we can assign Antiochus to Middle Platonism, and if we can, more doubt about what can be attributed to him rather than to, say, Cicero. Philo unfortunately can hardly be said to have come to grips with the problem. We saw earlier that he believed that God shaped and controlled the world through the *Logos* which is the place of his thoughts. This might seem to argue for close control by God, and in fact we find in *Cher.* 128 a presentation of God who is portrayed as playing upon us who are his instruments through the *Logos*. Yet Philo also proclaims the freedom of the will in strong terms. (*Deus.* 47-8) In short, Philo, like a good Platonist, proclaims both Providence and moral responsibility, and then simply leaves it at that.

Plutarch we saw attacking Aristotle, though politely, for allocating too little concern for the world to God. But on another occasion we find him having to produce arguments against the Stoics lest it should appear that God's providence in fact leaves no room for freedom in the world. Here he is reduced to saying that the craftsman, God, intervenes to vary the expected order; otherwise he would be as redundant as a gardener concerned with irrigation in a plot of ground that is naturally irrigated. (*De Fac.* 927) Elsewhere he praises Plato for the 'admirable' solution to the problem of choice in Book Ten of the *Republic* ('The chooser is responsible, God is without blame'). It is obvious that no progress has been made over Plato, and it is clear, from *Def. Or.* 435f, that in Plutarch no progress will be made.

One of the more interesting contributions to the discussion of the problem of evil comes from Nicomachus. This acknowledges readily that men suffer evils in the world. Moreover, they do this in accordance with providence which shows its goodness by inflicting these very evils. For if all went well for men they would speedily come to believe in their own self-sufficiency and forget that the gods exist. But their sufferings are a reminder of their finitude and a warning to men to behave themselves. (see *Theol. Ar.* p 42,3ff) We do not know what stimulated this particular piece of reasoning in Nicomachus. The myth told by Aristophanes in the

Symposium comes to mind, but the suggestion is purely speculative. That it remained a popular argument can be seen from
Augustine's laments about the pains of childhood in the *Confessions.* (I,14, 23)

We turn finally to Alcinous and Apuleius. In Alcinous we find,
what we have now come to expect from him, a sober separation of
the elements of the problem and a valiant attempt to provide a
moderate solution. He says we must be free to merit moral praise
or blame. If we decide to take such and such an initial step, then a
whole sequence of actions will necessarily follow, and the sequence can be said to be fated. But the initial step is the sign of our
freedom. Alcinous again draws on Aristotle in this section and
particularly the discussion in the *Nicomachaean Ethics* on the establishment of routine methods of behaviour. Apuleius also draws
heavily on received opinion in his discussion of providence in *De
Platone* (I 12), but in the end we are not left much wiser on the
whole problem. In many ways this is the most disappointing area
in Middle Platonism.

We may conclude by noting briefly that, fated or not, man was
bound to strive for virtue. His end in life was to become like unto
God. Eudorus took over this exhortation from the *Theaetetus,* and
we need say no more than that it was never forgotten throughout
the remainder of Middle Platonism. It should be added that the
very grandeur of the ambition, combined with the repetition, con-
trived to give the formula in the end not only a tired appearance
but an empty sound. It required the genius of a Plotinus or an
Augustine to bring it back to life.

CHAPTER SIX

Plotinus and Neoplatonism

The fact that we talk of Neoplatonism, with overtones of a revival of Platonism, is a tribute above all to Plotinus (204-270 AD). Plotinus himself was not anxious to get credit for originality: he considered himself a Platonist, working in the spirit of the master. Nevertheless, Plotinus did bring in something new, or brought back to consciousness things half-forgotten, not least the conviction, apparent from his writings, of philosophy as a total way of life. The problems of philosophy were alive and demanding answers all the time, answers that had to come out from the self and not simply to be copied from some predecessors. That accounts partly for the feeling of originality that we have with Plotinus. Since he is unwilling simply to repeat faithfully some central 'Platonist' doctrines, we have with him a development as a result of which Plotinus himself in later years will be regarded as providing a basic corpus which can be systematised and scholasticised.

Plotinus also makes an impression of originality by the very way in which he has been preserved by Porphyry, his student and friend. Porphyry was devoted to Plotinus but that luckily did not lead him to tidy up the text unduly. His own well-developed individuality led him, perhaps, to appreciate all the more the eccentricities in Plotinus' style and to preserve them faithfully. He quotes from a letter to himself from Longinus to whom he has sent treatises of Plotinus. Longinus says, 'I think that now, with what you have sent me, I have everything, though in a very imperfect state, for the manuscript is exceeding faulty. I had expected our friend Amelius to correct the scribal errors, but he evidently had something better to do. The copies are quite useless to me ... ' Porphyry comments, 'His notion ... that the transcripts he acquired from Amelius were faulty sprang from his misunderstanding of Plotinus' style and phraseology; if there were ever any accurate copies, these were they, faithful reproductions from the author's own manuscript'. (Porphyry, *Life of Plotinus*, chapters 19 and 20)

Porphyry had explained, at the end of chapter 7, 'I myself, Porphyry of Tyre, was one of Plotinus' very closest friends, and it
was to me he entrusted the task of revising his writings'. Porphyry continues (ch 8): 'Such revision was necessary: Plotinus
could not bear to go back on his work even for one re-reading;
and indeed the condition of his sight would scarcely allow it: his
handwriting was slovenly; he misjoined his words; he cared nothing about spelling; his one concern was for the idea: in these
habits, to our general surprise, he remained unchanged to the
very end. He used to work out his design mentally from first to
last: when he came to set down his ideas, he wrote out at one jet
all he had stored in mind as though he were copying from a book'.
And later on (ch 14) he reports: 'In style Plotinus is concise, dense
with thought, terse, more lavish of ideas than of words, most often expressing himself with a fervid inspiration. He followed his
own path rather than that of tradition ...'

It was certainly a lucky accident that someone like Porphyry
did come along to preserve the works of Plotinus, and our estima-
tion of him as compared to Numenius should be conditioned by
the fact that Numenius had not the same luck. Nevertheless, Plotinus was an extraordinary man and his reputation with posterity
does not rest on his handwriting or spelling. Porphyry's *Life of
Plotinus* is written by someone whom Plotinus had saved from
death by suicide. But even when allowance is made for that, and
for the reverential tone in which the life is written, it still gives a
convincing portrait of a personality as powerful as that of Socrates, even though Plotinus was more obviously intense and less inclined to make his points through jokes and general mockery. Yet
Plotinus, though intense, was serene: he was like a man who lived
at a level above that of the normal human being. Porphyry starts
his life by saying that 'Plotinus, the philosopher our contemporary, seemed ashamed of being in the body'. He goes on to report
that four times during the period he was with him, Plotinus
achieved a form of mystical unity with God. And yet Plotinus was
also obviously a highly competent man in ordinary business affairs and Porphyry also reports that a number of prominent men
and women in Rome left their children in his care and he made
sure that the accounts were properly kept. Prominent people also
formed part of his following which Porphyry tells us was large.
He had settled in Rome at the age of forty after an abortive
attempt to find out more about Persian and Indian philosophy.
He had started philosophy in Alexandria under Ammonius and
wrote in Greek.[1]

Plotinus had composed twenty one treatises when Porphyry first met him. Porphyry eventually set all the treatises in order, dividing them according to related topics into six sets of nine, 'an arrangement which pleased me by the happy combination of the perfect number six with the nines'. But he also has preserved the chronological order of the appearance of the treatises so that there is at least a possibility of estimating a development in Plotinus' thought. However that may be, there is from first to last an extraordinary insistence on life as a process of growing like to God. His system, as Dodds has said, (art. cit.141) has started from the transcendent theology of the *Parmenides* and the *Republic*, and proceeds upon the Platonic principles that like is known by like and that the goal of man is likeness to God insofar as that is possible. But the call for likeness is utterly transformed from Middle Platonism where, with a few exceptions, one has the impression of the dutiful repetition of a formula. The desire to grow like to God is the very life blood of Plotinus' philosophy and keeps recurring in the most unexpected surroundings.

For it should be emphasised that, while undoubtedly the religious urge is central to Plotinus' philosophy, he is still in the philosophical tradition. His seminars were not prayer meetings: he was always ready to entertain objections and Porphyry himself kept him going for three days running as to how the soul is associated with the body. (*Life* ch 13) Plotinus obviously knew the philosophical tradition even if he did not feel enchained by it. Porphyry again reports: 'At the Conferences he used to have treatises by various authors read aloud – among the Platonists it might be Severus or Cronius, Numenius, Gaius or Atticus; and among the Peripatetics Aspasius, Alexander, Adrastus, or some such writer, at the call of the moment'. (ch 14) The Stoic and Peripatetic doctrines in general are to be found in his work, Porphyry says. But as regards them all he adds, 'It was far from his way to follow any of these authors blindly; he took a personal, original view'.

That we shall see as we turn back now to the writings themselves.[2] This is a case where there can be no doubt that what is of particular interest to us is also central to Plotinus. He is concerned with the way to God, from first to last. The first treatise in the chronological series is I. 6, *On Beauty*. This treatise draws on favourite passages from Plato: the ascent to the Beautiful in the *Symposium*, the *Phaedrus* and of course the passage in the *Theaetetus* on becoming like to God. He begins by showing that we all accept that various forms of beauty exist, even if we cannot agree on a definition of beauty. So then, he says, 'Let us go back to the source, and indicate at once the principle that bestows beauty on material things'. He continues, 'Undoubtedly this Principle exists; it is something that is perceived at the first glance, something which the soul names as from an ancient knowledge and, recognising, welcomes it, enters into unison with it'. (I. 6.2) The beauty of this First Principle has left its mark everywhere in the universe and so draws us back to Itself, so that we might enjoy beauty in its perfection. 'Therefore we must ascend again towards the Good, the desired of every soul' .(I. 6.7) There are levels in the universe and the body is on the lowest level. At the highest level there is the Good, the One, the First. 'And Beauty, this beauty which is also The Good, must be posed as The First: directly deriving from this First is the Intellectual Principle (*nous* in Greek) which is preeminently the manifestation of Beauty, and through the Intellectual Principle soul is beautiful. The beauty in things of a lower order – actions and pursuits for instance – comes by operation of the shaping soul which is also the author of the beauty found in the world of sense. For the soul, a divine thing, a fragment as it were of the Primal Beauty, makes beautiful to the fullness of their capacity all things whatsoever that it grasps and molds'. (I. 6.6) We have there mentioned the four levels in the Plotinian universe, with the unchanging One or Good at the top, followed by *nous*, soul and the world.

We go to God because we are from God. An earlier tractate in the first *Ennead* (I. 2, or 19 in the chronological order, headed *On the Virtues*) starts by quoting from the *Theaetetus* passage on likeness to God. 'We must escape hence'. 'Our concern is not merely to be sinless but to be God'. (I. 2.6) And, as an indication that Plotinus never changed his position, we may quote from the last tractate in the chronological order, I .7, *On the First Good and the other goods*, where we are told once again (I. 7.1 13f) that 'all aspiration and Act whatsoever are directed towards the Good'. This tractate, his last, is also useful as giving an account in summary form of the related position which remained unchanged, the emergence of all things from the Good or the One. Plotinus is taking up a problem which arises from the postulation, in Plato and Aristotle, of a transcendent God who is perfect and unchanging: how or why does the imperfect changing world we know exist? Plotinus says, in language which combines the *Republic* of Plato and the *Metaphysics* of Aristotle: 'If all aspiration and act whatsoever are directed towards the Good, it follows that the Essential Good neither need nor can look outside itself or aspire to anything other than itself: it can but remain unmoved, as being, in the constitution of things,

the wellspring and first cause of all Act: whatsoever in other entities is of the nature of Good cannot be due to any Act of the essential Good upon them; it is for them on the contrary to act towards
their source and cause. The Good must, then, be the Good not by
an Act, not even by virtue of its Intellection, but by its very rest
within Itself. Existing beyond and above (*epekeina*) Being, it must
be beyond and above act and beyond and above the Intellectual
Principle and all Intellection. For, again, that only can be named
the Good to which all is bound and itself to none: for only this is it
veritably the object of all aspiration. It must be unmoved, while all
circles round it, as a circumference around a centre from which all
the radii proceed. Another example would be the sun, central to
the light that streams from it and is yet linked to it, or at least is always about it, irremovably; try all you will to separate the light
from the sun, or the sun from its light, forever the light is in the
sun'. (I. 7.1) The active mind is at a lower level than the One or the
Good in order to emphasise that the Supreme is unchanging.

There is, then, in the universe of Plotinus, an outgoing from the
Good and a return to it. But we note how he emphasises that the
Good is not changed by this outgoing. The Good is beyond everything. The Middle Platonic insistence on the unchanging nature of
God and on his ineffability seems moderate, even tentative, when
set beside that of Plotinus. He returns again and again to the
theme: only some of the passages can be quoted as illustration.
When we speak of the One and when we speak of The Good we
must recognise an identical nature; we must affirm that they are
the same – not, it is true, as venturing any prediction with regard
to that (unknowable) *Hypostasis* but simply as indicating it to ourselves in the best terms we find'. (II. 9.1) 'The One, as transcending Intellect, transcends knowing ... The One is in truth beyond
all statement: any affirmation is of a thing; but 'all transcending,
resting above even the most august divine Mind' this is the only
true description, since it does not make it a thing among things,
nor name it where no name could identify it: we can but try to indicate, in our own feeble way, something concerning it'. (V. 3
12dl3) 'We can and do state what it is not, while we are silent as to
what it is: we are, in fact, speaking of it in the light of sequels; unable to state it, we may still possess it'. (V. 3.14) 'We are in agony
for a true expression; we are talking of the untellable; we name,
only to indicate for our own use as best we may. And this name,
The One, contains really no more than the negation of plurality ...
If we are led to think positively of The One, name and thing, there
would be more truth in silence'. (V. 5.6) 'Our inquiry obliges us to

use terms not strictly applicable ... Once more, we must be patient with language; we are forced for reasons of exposition to apply to the Supreme terms which strictly are ruled out; everywhere we must read 'so to speak'.' (VI. 8.13)

In V. 1 Plotinus endeavours to discover traces of his own system in his predecessors. He comes to Aristotle and says of him: 'he begins by making the First transcendent and intellective, but cancels that primacy by supposing it to have self-intellection'.[9] Even intellection must be placed outside the One. After his fairly lengthy criticism of Aristotle he sets out briefly once again his own system: 'There exists a principle which transcends Being; this is the One, whose nature we have sought to establish in so far as such matters lend themselves to proof. Upon the One follows immediately the Principle which is at once Being and the Intellectual Principle (*nous*). Third comes the Principle, Soul'.[10] In V. 2 immediately following on this tractate (10 and 11 in the chronological order), Plotinus explains how this First Principle, which is so utterly remote, nevertheless is that to which the whole world is bound. 'Seeking nothing, possessing nothing, lacking nothing, the One is perfect and, in our metaphor, has overflowed, and its exuberance has produced the new: this product has turned again to its begetter and been filled and has become its contemplator and so an Intellectual Principle ... That vision directed upon the One establishes the Intellectual Principle; ... and, attaining resemblance in virtue of this vision, it repeats the act of the One in pouring forth a vast power. This second outflow is an image or representation of the Divine Intellect as the Divine Intellect represented its own prior, The One. This active power sprung from essence is Soul. Soul arises as the idea and act of the motionless Intellectual Principle – which itself sprang from its own motionless prior – but the Soul's operation is not similarly motionless; its image is generated from its movements. It takes fullness by looking to its source; but it generates its image by adopting another, a downward, movement. This image of Soul is Sense and Nature, the vegetal principle'. (V. 2.1)

That, in outline, is how the world has come into being: through an overflow, an outpouring, a circumradiation. We still do not know why. Plotinus explains by calling on the same stock of ideas from which he has drawn the how. He goes back to Plato's *Timaeus* and the passage on the upgrading nature of God (29E): 'How could the most perfect remain self set – the First Good, the Power towards all, how could it grudge or be powerless to give of itself, and how at that would it still be the Source?'. (V. 4.1) So goodness flows outwards, like light from the sun, heat from fire, cold from snow, water from a spring, a tree from its root. *Nous* looks back to the One, and wanting to imitate It, make something like It, it brings forth Soul. Soul in turn, in love with *nous*, brings forth the world, 'When living things reproduce their kind, it is that the Reason Principles (*logoi*) within stir them; the procreative act is the expression of a contemplation, a travail towards the creation of many forms, many objects of contemplation, so that the universe may be filled full with Reason Principles and that contemplation may be, as nearly as possible, endless: to bring anything into being is to produce an Idea-Form and that again is to enrich the universe with contemplation: all the failures, alive in being and in doing, are but the swerving of visionaries from the object of vision: in the end the sorriest craftsman is still a maker of forms, ungracefully. So Love, too, is vision with the pursuit of Ideal Form'. (III. 8.7)

The reference to 'failures', *hamartiai*, in this passage is an indication of the next problem which must be faced in the system of Plotinus. This is, if there is so much good in and above the world, how are we to explain the existence of evil? Plotinus devotes one of his last (chronologically, 51) tractates to the question, but of course does not confine himself to just that chapter. Like all previous thinkers be found the question difficult to answer, but with his metaphysical optimism and serene temperament he is not inclined to agonise over the problem. Evil is the contrary to Good, he tells us in I. 8, so to understand evil we have to do our best to understand Good. When we have done that we see that Evil has no place in the untroubled, blissful life of the three highest beings, the Good, *nous* and the Soul. Evil then must be some form of Non Being, something turned away from Being. Plotinus explains (I. 8.7): 'Given that The Good is not the only existent thing, it is inevitable that, by the outgoing from it or, if the phrase be preferred, the continuous down going or away going from it, there should be produced a Last, something after which nothing more can be produced: this will be Evil'. This is a very intriguing notion and we may linger a little on it. Lack of measure, indetermination, are bad things, according to Plotinus: the goodness in things is due to their form (see II. 5.5;III. 4.1). But there comes a point, apparently, when form can no longer impose itself. As Plotinus puts it elsewhere (IV. 3.9): 'While the Soul is at rest – in rest firmly based on Repose, the Absolute – yet, as we may put it, that huge illumination of the Supreme pouring outwards comes at last to the extreme bourne of its light and dwindles to darkness: this darkness, now lying there beneath, the Soul sees and by seeing brings to shape; for in the law of things this ultimate depth, neighbouring with soul, may not go void of whatsoever degree of that Reason. Principle it can absorb, the dimmed reason of reality at its faintest'. This would seem to imply that whatever exists, having form, has goodness; therefore the material world that we experience is good, in spite of the intrusion of evil.

But how is evil allowed to intrude? It is apparently due to the willfulness of the lower soul. Plotinus explains in the treatise on the origin of evil (I. 8), which we have been following, that 'The Soul wrought to perfection, addressed towards the Intellectual Principle is steadfastly pure: it has turned away from matter; all that is undertermined, that is outside of measure, that is evil, it neither sees nor hears ... The Soul that breaks away from the source of its reality, in so far as it is not perfect or primal, is, as it were, a secondary, an image to the loyal soul. By its falling away – and to the extent of the fall – it is stripped of Determination, becomes wholly indeterminate, sees darkness. Looking to what repels vision, as we look when we are said to see darkness it has taken Matter to itself'. [4]

But we still want to know: why did the latter soul break away? Plotinus tells us that, at the time decreed, 'The souls peering forth from the Intellectual Realm descend first to the heaven and these put on a body; this becomes at once the medium by which as they reach out more and more towards magnitude (physical extension) they proceed to bodies progressively more earthy. Some even plunge from heaven to the very lowest of corporeal forms; others pass, stage by stage, too feeble to lift towards the higher the burden they carry, weighed downwards by their heaviness and forgetfulness'. (IV. 3.15) Or, as he says at I. 8.14: 'The illumination, the light streaming from the Soul, is dulled, is weakened, as it mixes with Matter which offers birth to the Soul, providing the means by which it enters into generation, impossible to it if no recipient were at hand. This is the fall of the Soul, this entry into Matter: thence its weakness: not all the faculties of its being retain free play, for Matter hinders their manifestation; it encroaches upon the Soul's territory and, so it were, crushes the Soul back; and it turns to evil all that it has stolen, until the Soul finds strength to advance again'. More precisely, he asks in V. 1.1: 'What can it be that has brought souls to forget the father, god, and though members of the Divine and entirely of that world, to ignore at once themselves and It?' And he answers: 'The evil that has overtaken them has its source in self will, in the entry into the sphere of process, and in the primal differentiation with the desire for self ownership. They conceived pleasure in this freedom and largely indulged their own motion; thus they were hurried down the wrong path ...' Similarly in III. 9.3: 'Movement towards the lower is towards non Being: and this is the step the soul takes when it is set on self; for by willing towards itself it produces its lower, an image of itself – a non Being – and so is wandering, as it were, into the void, stripping itself of its own determined form ... As long as it remains at the mid-stage it is in its own peculiar region; but when, by a sort of inferior orientation, it looks down-ward, it shapes that lower image and flings itself joyfully thither'.

We are to think then, as he says at IV. 8.7, of the Soul as an inter-mediate, the upper Soul in uninterrupted contemplation of the world of the Forms and the lower involved in the shaping and ad-ministration of the universe. The individual soul can go astray through selfishness, through being absorbed with its own handi-work, whenever, as he says, 'it plunges in an excessive zeal to the very midst of its chosen sphere; then it abandons its status as whole soul with whole soul'. (ibid) But even in this descent into evil Plotinus can see good, for he goes on to say that the soul by its experience of evil can come to a clearer perception of Good. It is Plotinus' optimism, above all, which allows him to rest content with this explanation of the soul's turning to evil, just as it is his optimism which helps him to justify the ways of God to man. He puts forward various arguments of the type we have seen before, but set within the frame of his own thought. So, for instance, in the first treatise on Providence (III. 2), he says: 'The conflict and destruction that reign among living beings are inevitable since things here are derived, brought into existence because the Divine Reason which contains all of them in the upper Heavens ... must outflow over the whole extent of Matter'. As a result 'the very wronging of man by man may be derived from an effort towards the Good; foiled, in their weakness, of their true desire, they turn against each other'. (III. 2.4) So we must judge in terms of the whole: 'It is impossible to condemn the whole on the merits of the parts which, besides, must be judged only as they enter harmoni-ously or not into the whole, the main consideration, quite over passing the members which thus cease to have importance'. (III. 2.3) 'Accidents are not without their service in the co-ordination and completion of the Universal system. One thing perishes, and the Cosmic Reason – whose control nothing anywhere eludes – employs that ending to the beginning of something new'. 'Once the wrong has come to be, the Reason of the Cosmos employs it to

good ends'. (III. 2.5).Wrong doing appears to be a necessary concomitant of freedom. 'Such living beings as have freedom of motion under their own will sometimes take the right turn, sometimes the wrong'. (III. 2.4) Within this context, Plotinus serenely
continues, 'Why the wrong course is followed is scarcely worth
inquiring: a slight deviation at the beginning develops with every
advance into a continuously wider and graver error – especially
since there is the attached body with its inevitable concomitant of
desire – and the first step, the hasty movement not previously
considered and not immediately corrected, ends by establishing a
set habit where there was at first only a fall'. (III. 2.4) Therefore,
'once happiness is possible at all to souls in this Universe, if some
fail of it, the blame must fall not upon the place but upon the feebleness insufficient to the staunch combat in the one area where
the rewards of excellence are offered'. (III. 2.5) Plotinus is a believer in self help: decent people who have not attempted to train
themselves for life no more deserve pity than pampered boys
who are set on by a gang of young thugs in the gymnasium and
have their clothes and nice food stolen. 'Bad men rule by the feebleness of the ruled: and this is just'. (III. 2.8)

But the old problem still remains: why do the evil prosper and
the good suffer? There is a series of connected answers to this.
Firstly, we must remember: 'Men are not born divine; what wonder that they do not enjoy a divine life. And poverty and sickness
mean nothing to the good, while to the evil they bring benefit:
where there is body there must be ill health'. (III. 2.5) 'Some of
these troubles are helpful to the very sufferers – poverty and sickness, for example – and as for vice, even this brings something to
the general service: it acts as a lesson in right doing, and, in many
ways even, produces good; thus, by setting men face to face with
the ways and consequences of iniquity, it calls them from lethar-
gy, stirs the deeper mind, and sets the understanding to work; by
the contrast of the evil under which wrong-doers labour it dis-
plays the worth of the right'. (III. 2.5) We simply must take the
overall view. 'The Reason Principle (logos) is the sovereign, making all: it wills things as they are and, in its reasonable act, it produces even what we know as evil: it cannot desire all to be good:
an artist would not make an animal all eyes ... We are like people
ignorant of painting who complain that the colours are not beautiful everywhere in the picture: but the Artist has laid on the appropriate tint to every spot ... We are censuring a drama because the
persons are not all heroes but include a servant and a rustic and
some scurrilous clown; yet take away the low character and the

power of the drama is gone; these are part and parcel of it'. (See further section 15, and cf. II. 3.18) We may conclude this section with a striking passage from the treatise against the Gnostics, II. 9: 'The natural movement within the plan will be injurious to any-thing whose natural tendency it opposes: one group will sweep bravely onward with the great total to which it is adopted; the others, not able to comply with the larger order, are destroyed. A great choral is moving to its concerted plan; midway in the march, a tortoise is intercepted; unable to get away from the choral line it is trampled under foot; but if it could only range itself within the greater movement it too would suffer nothing'.

Evil is obvious, but so is Providence: Plotinus in fact argues that the existence of apparent evil is even demanded by the neces-sary existence of Providence. We have to work to defend our-selves against the wicked. We have seen that 'bad men rule by the feebleness of the ruled: and this is just'. He continues: 'The triumph of weaklings would not be just. It would not be just be-cause Providence cannot be a something reducing us to nothing-ness: to think of Providence as everything, with no other thing in existence is to annihilate Providence itself since it could have no field of action; nothing would exist except the Divine'. (III. 2.8.9) The world is planned by God, but man is free. Plotinus again is so convinced of the fact that man is free to do his best, free to be di-vine, that he does not waste time in arguing the point. And that the world is planned by God, planned in the sense of emanating from him and brought into order by the Forms in his Mind and through the agency of Soul, is central to his system, conveniently summarised in II. 3.17 and 18: 'Creation is the operation of that phase of the Soul which contains Ideal Principles; for that is its strongest puissance, its creative part. It creates, then, on the model of the Forms; for, what it has received from the Intellectual Princi-ple it must pass on in turn. In sum, then, the Intellectual Principle gives from itself to the Soul of the All which follows immediately upon it: this again gives forth from itself to its next, illuminated and imprinted by it; and that secondary Soul at once begins to create, as under order, unhindered in some of its creations, striv-ing in others against the repugnance of Matter' ... 'The Soul of the All abides in contemplation of the Highest and Best, ceaselessly striving towards the Intelligible Kind and towards god: but, thus absorbing and filled full, it overflows – so to speak – and the im-age it gives forth, its last utterance towards the lower, will be the creative puissance ... Rightly, therefore, is this Cosmos described as an image continuously being imaged, the First and Second

Principles immobile, the Third, too, immobile essentially, but accidentally and in Matter, having motion. For as long as divine Mind and Soul exist, the divine Ideal Principles (*logoi*) or Thought-Forms will pour forth into that phase of the Soul: as long as there is a sun, all that streams from it will be some form of Light'.

But light needs the source of light, and in conscious beings the principle of light wishes to return to its origin. In a sense it has always remained with the origin: as Plotinus says, not all soul is descended: but when it is quickened by the consciousness of beauty and seized with longing, it begins the process of returning entire to the One. This is the flight from evil, the purification of the Soul, the likening to God. The world is beautiful, but it is only the image of an image of an image. Our true self belongs above. 'Soul, that soul which as possessing knowledge and vision was capable, clung to what it saw; and as its vision so its rapture; it saw and was stricken; but having in itself something of that principle it felt its kinship and was moved to longing like those stirred by the image of the beloved to desire of the veritable presence. Lovers here mould themselves to the beloved; they seek to increase their attraction of person and their likeness of mind; they are unwilling to fall short in moral quality or in other graces lest they be distasteful to those possessing such merit – and only among such can true love be. In the same way the soul loves the Supreme Good, from its very beginnings stirred by it to love. The soul which has never strayed from this love waits for no reminding from the beauty of our world: holding that love – perhaps unawares – it is ever in quest, and, in its longing to be borne thither, passes over what is lovely here and with one glance at the beauty of the universe dismisses all. By only noting the flux of things it knows at once that from elsewhere comes the beauty that floats upon them and so it is urged thither, passionate in pursuit of what it loves: never – unless someone robs it of that love – never giving up till it attains. There indeed all it saw was beautiful and veritable; it grew in strength by being thus filled with the life of the True; itself becoming veritable being and attaining veritable knowledge, it enters by that neighbouring into conscious possession of what it has long been seeking'. (VI. 7.31)

We saw, when talking of the life of Plotinus, that Porphyry reports that four times while he was with him Plotinus experienced some form of mystical unity with God. And in a tractate written before Porphyry met him, IV. 8, chronologically number 6, Plotinus says: 'Many times it has happened: lifted out of the body into myself; becoming external to all other things and self-encentred;

beholding a marvellous beauty; then, more than ever, assure of community with the loftiest order; enacting the noblest life, acquiring identity with the diverse; stationing within It by having attained that activity; poised above whatever within the Intellectual is less than the Supreme'.[1] The tractate is on the Soul's Descent into Body, and in turning to his topic after this introduction, Plotinus says, 'Yet, there comes the moment of descent from intellection to reasoning' (*eis logismon ek nou*). We have just seen the description of the ascent of the soul to the Supreme in VI .7.51. Shortly after that we have the picture of the soul in possession of the object of her longing. Plotinus obviously thinks that the purpose of philosophy is a form of unity with the One which we call mystical. He compares it elsewhere (VI. 9.10) to the superimposition of the centres of concentric circles. We cannot quote all the description in VI. 7, but section 34 should be read. He continues in section 35: 'Such in this union is the soul's temper that even the act of Intellect once so intimately loved she now dismisses; Intellection is movement and she has no wish to move ... In this state of absorbed contemplation there is no longer question of holding an object: the vision is continuous so that seeing and seen are one thing; object and act of vision have becoming identical ... The soul attains that vision by – so to speak – compounding and annulling the Intellectual Principle within it'. In section 36 he turns back and describes once again the process of purification and intellectual preparation for the ascent to the Good to the point that 'we no longer see the Supreme as an external'. He continues: 'We are near now, the rest is That and it is close at hand, radiant above the Intellectual. Here we put aside all the learning; disciplined to this pitch, established in beauty, the quester holds knowledge still of the ground he rests on, but, suddenly, swept beyond it all by the very crest of the wave of Intellect surging beneath, he is lifted and sees, never knowing how; the vision floods the eyes with light, but it is not a light showing some other object, the light is itself the vision .With this he himself becomes identical, with that radiance whose Act is to engender intellectual principle not losing in that engendering but for ever unchanged, the engendered coming to be simply because that supreme exists'. And even with all this said it is inadequate; the vision cannot be communicated in words. (VI. 9.10) Even 'vision' itself is unsatisfactory, due to the fact that 'we cannot help talking in dualities'. As a consequence Plotinus sometimes prefers to talk of touching rather than seeing, the flight of the alone to the alone.

It was to be expected that a philosophy which culminates in

mystical union with God would have a great attraction for Christians who were either trying to persuade themselves intellectually of the God of their faith or were trying to make their faith intellectually respectable in the eyes of other people. Christians of this sort tended either to ignore the difficulties in Plotinus' position, or to acknowledge them as defects which Christianity had remedied. The mystical union itself could not be expected to be experienced 'many times' by the average Christian. And was the human being one uniting with a what or a whom? Plotinus in the traditional Greek manner spoke of his supreme being in both personal and neuter terms. But the man who did most to make 'Platonism', as he called it, part of Christianity, Augustine, was not deterred by these problems. 'Change a few words and they are Christians'. We shall turn to him in the next chapter but first we must consider the other Neoplatonists, beginning with Plotinus' friend and admirer, Porphyry.

We gather most of our knowledge of Prophyry himself from his *Life of Plotinus* with which he prefaced the *Enneads*, and from some of the other writings of his which have been preserved.He was a very voluminous writer and a great deal has been lost. Even what has been preserved is often in fragmentary form and demands, on occasion, reconstruction which in turn entails risk. He was born in the modern Lebanon and was not Greek by birth, though obviously Hellenised. His background meant that he had a range of knowledge and interests which were much broader, very often, than the Christians by whom he was later criticised. But his knowledge of things Jewish did not stand in the way of an education which was as good as that of any Greek of his day. He studied in Athens with Longinus where he would have broadened his knowledge of Platonism. But the most important year in his life was 263, when he came to Rome at the age of thirty and met Plotinus. His admiration of Plotinus we have already seen, but we have also seen that Porphyry did not accept everything that came from Plotinus simply at first hearing: here is his own story about how on one occasion he questioned Plotinus for three days, and he also reports how Plotinus charged another disciple to reply to Porphyry's written differences on an important point in Plotinian teaching. Plotinus obviously thought a great deal of him, and it was because of his advice to go way for a holiday that Porphyry was not present at Plotinus' death. He was in Sicily at that time but he will not have stayed there. He issued the *Enneads* about thirty years after the death of Plotinus, but his *Life* and edition of the *Enneads* represent only portion of his scholarly work and production in the seventy years or so he had now lived. We know from his own description that he was a restless person and not at all the pure speculative philosopher of the type of Plotinus. The range of his interests left its mark on his work, and it seems that in his enthusiasm he was able to combine views which others would have apart. Pophyry obviously believed that the truth was one and that all who thought truly belonged to the one school. It is significant that the work for which he was for centuries best known was an Introduction, the *Eisagoge*, not to the works of Plato or Plotinus, but to the *Categories* of Aristotle. He did not keep the traditions in watertight compartments, but nevertheless with his long and active life it is only prudent to attempt to distinguish phases or stages in the thought of Porphyry. This can be seen, for instance, in his attitude to Christianity. There we have at an early stage admiration for Christ, the most pious of men, though not well served by his disciples;[3] and at a later one, in *Against the Christians*, wide ranging criticism not just of the Old and New Testament, and particular disciples and evangelists, but of Christ himself. In discussing his theology, we can start by making a rough distinction between a pre-Plotinian, a Plotinian, and a post-Plotinian stage, though he would scarcely have made that distinction himself and we must always remember that Porphyry's generous interpretations tended to get him into difficulties with meticulous thinkers. Platonism in general is always strong in his theology: the question arises about his treatment of specifically Plotinian positions.

We can have various traditions in the same work, or in works written roughly at the same time. So for instance, even after the death of Plotinus he can be seen drawing on a theology which Plotinus would not have rejected but which could have been written even if Plotinus had never existed. We can see that in the *De Abstinentia*, written not much after 271, and which contains a theology which the Budé edition (p XXXIX) calls clearly pre-Plotinian. There he writes: 'If we want to return to that which is properly ours, we must abandon all that we have acquired under the influence of human nature and that which drags us towards there and which is responsible for our fall; we should remember the blessed and eternal being and make every effort to return to the being which is without colour and without quality.' (I. 30)

As the latest editors of the text in the Budé series say, this negative theology is characteristic of Middle Platonism and goes back to Plato himself, especially *Phaedrus* 247c. The direct Platonic influence is very obvious in II. 37 of the same writing where he talks of the first God, who is incorporeal, has no parts, and no need of anything outside himself.

But then he goes on to talk of the world soul, and visible gods, and there is a long discussion of daemons, good and evil, where it is suggested that Porphyry has been influenced by Numenius towards a dualism which no orthrodox Platonist should permit. Yet that this, if heresy, was not intended is to be seen from the consideration of a roughly contemporary work by Porphyry. The *Sentences* were also, according to their latest editor,[4] written a short rather than a long time after the death of Plotinus in view of their general Plotinian attitudes. (Lamberz L II) Porphyry tells us there, in *Sent*. 43, that the One comes first: *nous* cannot be the first principle, since it is also a many. The One contains everything 'non-intellectively and hyper-essentially'. (*Sent*. 10.) The One is not Being but beyond Being. (*Sent*. 26) All this is Plotinian enough.

And yet there is now fairly general agreement that, after the death of Plotinus also, Porphyry came under the influence of the *Chaldaean Oracles*, a collection put together in the century before Porphyry and which combined among other things Platonism, Stoicism and magic. It is further suggested by some scholars that under their influence he began to lessen the distance between the *Hypostases* of Plotinus and consequently to reduce the emphasis on the utter transcendence of the One. Lloyd, followed by Wallis, has talked of a tendency to telescope the *Hypostases*, and we are presented with a picture of the human being trying to raise himself up through his own *nous* into the presence of the One. Not all scholars would agree with this interpretation, and even among those who do, it is also commonly agreed that Porphyry was not necessarily aware of any unfaithfulness to Plotinus in this process, and that he was certainly not trying to abandon transcendence.[5] And if he escaped his own notice in his 'heresy', he also seems to have escaped that of the most influential Christians who used his writings, especially Ambrose and Augustine. To both of these he was congenial for his very religiosity, his efforts to turn the soul to the Highest by all possible means, including if necessary theurgy or the use of magic ritual to unite men and gods. Practical men like those who were interested in the salvation of Christians gladly accepted his moral urgings and exhortations that the soul should turn from what is below and return to what is above. The niceties of the question left them unmoved, as is very obvious particularly from Augustine. Augustine was quite willing to take Plotinus' teaching and Porphyry's 'heresy' together and point to the mixture proudly as a support for the Christian doctrine of the Trinity.

Other Neoplatonists were not so happy with the work of Porphyry as we can see from the reports of those who came after him. Iamblichus is a good example. He is not of such direct importance for the West as Porphyry, but he was revered in the Neoplatonic school as the great, the 'divine' Iamblichus, and had a very great influence on the successors in the school and particularly on Proclus who, through a process which we shall observe, did have an enormous impact on Western theological thinking. Iamblichus came from the same general area as Porphyry, from Syria, and was as Hellenised as he was. We know very little about his life, but it is reckoned that he was born about 242 and died about 326 AD. He was, therefore, a slightly younger contemporary of Porphyry and he certainly knew Porphyry's works, whether or not he knew Porphyry personally. He studied under Anatolius, later to be a Christian bishop, in Caesarea, and then, perhaps in the 280s, studied with Porphyry in Rome. He spent the last twenty years of his life teaching in his own school in Syria. Whether he was also physically in Alexandria does not matter very much to us: there can be no doubt that he would have been familiar with the philosophy pursued there.

He was, apparently, a more consistent thinker than Porphyry whom he criticises: Porphyry was the polymath, Iamblichus the philosopher. Apparently, I say, because we have only a relatively small portion of the work of each, and in the case of Iamblichus a good deal of it is preserved by Proclus who often quotes him as critical of Porphyry. This may indicate a general attitude of distrust of Porphyry's deviations from Plotinus (or Plato) and a rejection of the alleged telescoping of the *hypostases*, but it also simply indicates normal scholarly disagreement. We know that Iambilichus was critical of Porphyry's *Letter to Anebo* and wrote *De Mysteriis*, perhaps his earliest work, against it, but given Porphyry's inconsistency this incident is scarcely indicative of any great gap between them.

Like Porphyry, he was a very pious man, and regarded as the highest form of prayer the ineffable uniting with the gods, making our soul rest in them. (*De Myst*. 238,3ff) We strive upwards even though we are deeply conscious of the mystery of divine activity. There can be no question of any wavering on the part of Iamblichus about the utter transcendence of the supreme. He was consistent, a systematiser, the first of the Neoplatonist scholastics. He was loyal to the system of Plotinus, but felt that it should be further developed and rendered impregnable to attack. The emanation, the outflowing, and the return which characterised the

system had to be retained, but in such a way as not to endanger
the utter transcendence of the One. And so Iamblichus elaborated
a system, the germ of which is to be seen in Plotinus' description
of the two-fold soul. For Plotinus not all soul will run the risk of
being contaminated by the matter which it must order and control. A part of it will always remain looking upwards. Iamblichus
elaborated this, so that as we move upwards in his scale of being
we come to The One existent, *To Hen On*. But this is only the peak
of the realm of *nous*. Before we reach the absolute peak we have to
pass upwards through the area of Limit and the Unlimited, to the
Second One, called the Simply One, and finally to the first One,
the completely ineffable. (*Damascius Dub, et Sol*. I, 103 6ff. Ruelle)
If there had been the slightest danger of diminishing God's transcendence in Porphyry, the danger was now removed through
Iamblichus, and later Neoplatonism, which is dependent on Iamblichus, will insist more and more on transcendence.

The most important figure in this later Neoplatonism was Proclus, who has preserved for us a great deal of Iamblichus together
with the opinions of other philosophers because he too was above
all a Neoplatonist scholastic. He lists his heroes for us in the first
chapter of the *Platonic Theology*: first of all comes Plato himself, the
guide to the mysteries and hierophant, and then Plotinus the
Egyptian and those who have had the doctrine passed on from
him, Amelius and Porphyry, and in the third place those wonderful men, like Iamblichus and Theodorus,who have learned from
them. He is unmistakably a Platonist: 'The truth about the gods is
spread (one might say), through all of the dialogues of Plato'. (*Pr*
I. p 23.22ff), even though the *Parmenides* takes pride of place as
the specifically theological dialogue. Proclus wrote a special commentary on the *Parmenides* and in the course of it gives a history of
the interpretation of the *Parmenides* which is a sufficient indication of his awareness of the tradition. This, and the volume of his
writings, would be reason enough for us to choose him as a representative later Neoplatonist. But we choose him also because, as
we shall see, one of the most influential of Christian writers, Pseudo-Dionysius, appears to rely very heavily on Proclus. Besides
this, there is the *Liber de Causis*, a translation of an Arabic work of
the ninth century based on Proclus' *Elements of Theology*, one of
the most important 'theological' works for medieval scholasticism. These writings, and those of Maximus the Confessor and
John of Damascus (d c 750 AD), were the channels of Prochus'
enormous influence on medieval Christian theologians who
shaped the teaching on God (*De Deo Uno*) which has remained vir-
tually unchanged in the main Christian churches until now.

Proclus was born in 412 in Constantinople and saw different cities before coming to Athens in 430. He had already made the preparatory studies in mathematics and Aristotelian philosophy, and now was able to have the benefit of the great Platonists. He heard Plutarch, who died in 432, and then studied further with Syrianus, who died perhaps in 437, before becoming himself head of the school. He wrote to excess, but luckily for us wrote two works which have the advantage of being systematic, and, in the case of the *Elements of Theology* at least, comparatively brief. The *Elements* is regarded as a fairly early work and the *Platonic Theology* was a somewhat later one but as there are no great variations in the body of his work we may draw on them indiscriminately. As we read them we see how much Proclus is interpreting Plato from Plotinus, and what a faithful Neoplatonist he is. We find, for instance, the basic structure in ascending order of body-soul-*nous*-One. (*ET*. 20) That which is primarily good is beyond (*epekeina*) beings. (*ET* 8) The Good is identical with the One. (*ET* 13) 'That the One is God follows from its identity with the good: for the Good is identical with God, God being that which is beyond (*epekeina*) all things and to which all things aspire'. (*ET* 113. Dodds' trs.) He tells us in the *Platonic Theology* that Plato's first principle totally transcends *nous* and is ineffable. (*PT* I 3 p 13.20ff) Our goal should be to collect ourselves in peace and make contact 'with the Ineffable which is beyond (*epekeina*) all beings'. (ibid. p 16.20ff) He gives a perfectly orthodox Plotinian exposition of permanence, procession and return. (*PT* II 6 p 41.18ff; I 18 p 84)

Proclus insists so much on the transcendence of the One that he runs the usual danger of seeming to make God remote from and unconcerned with the world. But he insists that, though God is ineffable and unknowable, Plato has nevertheless shown us the ways towards him and has succeeded in creating a developed theology. The ways to him that Proclus points to are those of analogy and of negation. (*PT* II 5 p 37) The *Republic* is particularly important for the first with the analogy of the Sun, and the *Parmenides* for the second. The two ways complement one another: Proclus has earlier (ibid. II 4) shown, against Amelius, 'that the very first cause is beyond *nous* and transcends all beings' in the view of Plato, Plotinus and Porphyry, and for Plato's views he adduces the *Republic*, *Sophist*, *Philebus* and *Parmenides*.

Plato has different manners of teaching about divine topics, he says (*PT* I. 4), and from him we learn the important attributes of the gods. The divine is unchanging and free from deceit, good and true. (*PT* I 17) The gods are omniscient and their omniscience includes the infinity of future contingents, they are wise and beautiful (*PT* I. 21-24), divine, immortal, intelligible, unitary, indissoluble, unchanging (*PT* I.26-27). Time and again Proclus repeats that the gods are good, the cause of all good and no evil, and that their providence never fails. (*PT* I. 15-18) He repeats Amelius' notion of a Form of Evil, and the views of Plutarch and Atticus on an evil soul in the universe. (*PT* I 18 p 87) The cause of evil is the weakness of those receiving the good. (I 18 p 86)

Proclus' theology is, then, optimistic. Evil is simply the absence of good and has no real existence. (*PT* I 18; *Mal. Subs.* 50-4) He describes in exalted terms the voyage of the soul towards the One on the way of negation. (*PT* II 11) 'Every being, entering into that which is ineffable in its own nature, discovers the symbol of the Father of the whole universe.' (*PT* II 8 p 56 20f) He brings together in the passage the themes of the return and the likening to God. It is by silence, he says, that we should celebrate the ineffability of the One. (II 9 p 58.23f) It is a silence which he himself did not observe and, as a result, exercised a very great influence on his Christian successors.

CHAPTER SEVEN

Three Christian Philosophers

In the preface I announced my intention of concentrating on the theology of the pagan philosophers down to the time when the philosophers themselves became Christian. Proclus lived and died a pagan, and there were to be many distinguished pagan philosophers after him who concerned themselves with theology. But by the time he died, in 485 AD, three men had appeared who showed what direction the philosophy of religion was to take. Admittedly, the last of these, Boethius, was only a child when Proclus died. But the first of them, Marius Victorinus, was born just a few years after Plotinus died, and the Platonic influence transmitted through Marius to the middle man, Augustine, has given rise to a discussion which still goes on about whether men like Augustine became converted to Platonism or Christianity. All three certainly illustrate, as I said before, how congenial Platonism was to Christianity and will be considered simply as philosophers who happened to be or became Christians and who, through their philosophy, helped to give Christian theology what might be called its classic shape in the works of Thomas Aquinas

Marius Victorinus has been called 'the one great link between Greek philosophy and the Latin world in the fourth century'.[1] Because of the place of St Augustine in Christian thought, Victorinus can also be called the link between Greek philosophy and Christian theology. Augustine explains in the *Confessions* how impressed he was with the teaching of Ambrose and 'the books of Platonists' which he had happened to come across, and how he was sent to the old priest Simplicianus for further instruction. He continues (8,2,3), 'When I told him that I had read certain books of the Platonists which had been translated into Latin by Victorinus, one-time professor of Rhetoric in Rome – who had, so I heard, died a Christian – he congratulated me for not having fallen upon the writings of other philosophers which are full of vain deceits whereas, in the Platonists, God and his Word are everywhere implied'. Simplicianus then went on to tell him the story of Victorinus. 'Here was an old man deeply learned, trained in all the liberal sciences, a man who had read and weighed so many of the philosophers' writings'. 'He had grown old in the worship of idols', and yet when he finally came to read the scriptures and 'all the Christian writings', he became a believer in Christianity and eventually made a public profession of faith which astounded Rome.

This had happened about thirty years before the time when Augustine was talking to Simplicianus. It is reckoned that Victorinus was born about 275 AD and became a Christian about 355. Jerome tells us that he wrote 'extremely obscure books, understood only by the learned'.[2] We have writings from him concerned mainly with Trinitarian questions, even if we do not have his translations of the books of the Platonists to which Augustine refers. But the theological works we do have are sufficient indication of how much Christian thought had become impregnated by Platonism at this time. He must have started writing these works about 357 AD which means, if his supposed date of birth is correct, that he was then over eighty. Even if we were to base our conjectures on his age at the time of his Christian writings, it would seem not unreasonable to presume that there was no considerable development in his thought. So I shall quote from his writings without any reference to comparative chronology. I shall also take with Victorinus a correspondent of his called Candidus, not in an attempt to harmonise their views on the finer points of Trinitarian theology, but merely as a demonstration of how close their views were on theological matters which had been dealt with by the pagans who preceded them.

So, for instance, Candidus and Victorinus are agreed that God is one and alone, being, living and intelligising, without beginning or end, therefore infinite, therefore incomprehensible, unknowable, unchanging. Victorinus says that to talk about God is a form of daring which is beyond man: to know the unspeakable mysteries of the wishes or acts of God is difficult, and to ennunciate them is impossible. (AC 1 5ff) God is above all the things that are and all the things that are not, even though, he adds, we believe that God is that which *is* rather than that which is not. (AC 2 16 ff) This rather strange statement has to be understood against the background of Victorinus' division of existents. He says (AC 5) that there are four modes of existence or levels of being: 1) truly existents, 2) existents, 3) not truly non-existents, 4) non-existents.

He explains then (AC 7) what are the truly existents and we discover that there is an ascending order also here. We move upwards from a) the supracelestials, and as sample of these are given the spirit, *nous*, soul, knowledge, *disciplina*, the virtues, *logoi*, opinions, perfection, existence, life, intelligence. Then above these, he says, come b) *existentialitas, vitalitas* and *intellegentitas*. Then above them all comes c) *on*, existence, which is the one and only existence.

The next level is that of the existents (only), and to this level belongs soul. Victorinus says we arrive at an understanding of the next two levels by turning down and away from the notion of being. Consequently the third level refers to the sensible world and that which gives it life, and the fourth to inanimate matter. But luckily we need not concern ourselves with these levels, and may return with gratitude to the highest, God, as Victorinus does in chapter 13 of the *Ad Candidum*. The discussion of the four modes of existence or levels of being has really been a digression necessary to explain why he said in chapter two that God is above all the things that are and all the things that are not. What then is God? Victorinus says now that 'God is above all existence, all life, all knowledge, above all being and the things that truly are, since he is unintelligible, infinite, invisible, inconceivable, insubstantial, unknowable, and because he is above all things, nothing of the things are ... God therefore is *me on*', he concludes, (using the Greek terms in the middle of his Latin) , non-existent.

This statement seems even more extraordinary than that which he set out to explain in chapter 2. So he explains further. God, the *me on*, the non-existent, is above the *on*, existent or being, but is not to be understood as either being or not being, but only as intelligible by ignorance, since he is both being and non-being. He is therefore to be described as *pro on*, or pre-being. Victorinus then turns to more strictly Christian theology and trinitarian discussions which we wish to avoid. But his prayer at he end of the *Ad Candidum* may be quoted as a mixture of Neoplatorism and Christianity which will become typical. 'Save us now, Father, and pardon our sins. And this very thing is a sin – to say about God what he is and how he is, and to use the human voice in an attempt to make statements about divine realities instead of adoring them. Yet, since you have given the spirit to us, we have and can express a partial knowledge of you, so that though we are in total ignorance about you, we have some knowledge of you ...' [3]

We can see already that Victorinus is very much in the tradition we have been examining. So also is his friend Candidus, and even more interestingly so, because of a long series of criticisms of the idea that God generates. Candidus is arguing in a Christian (Arian) context, but his criticisms are applicable to pagan Neoplatonic positions: indeed, one might argue that the roots of his thought are to be found at least in Plato's *Timaeus* and even in Parmenides himself. His basic position is if God is being and therefore unchanging, then there can be no talk of becoming associated with him. He then runs down through a list of possible solutions to, or evasions of, the dilemma of Parmenides, many of which have been mentioned here already in purely philosophical contexts, while some also combine explanations of the Trinity attempted by Christians.

First of all, he says, we cannot say that there is generation from God as these might be in the case where light is reflected (*iuxta effulgentiam*). For a reflection of this sort is a movement and therefore a separating of the light in question from its source, and therefore a change in the source. If this separation is confirmed, there is a division in the source. If the separation is not so confirmed, what is the point of it? A further point which is more of Trinitarian interest can be ignored here.

Nor may we think of generation from God as like the projection of a ray of light. For the ray is either an addition to the source or it is nothing. Nor may we think of it as like the flux of a point. For a point is unmoving, and neither has parts nor is part of anything else. Therefore there is no movement out from itself. Nor may we think of it as like an emission or projection in general. For this would mean either that there is a lessening of the source, or if the projection is of the same power as God, we have two equal perfections. And what is the point of that? Even perfections are not to be multiplied without necessity. And if the projection is not of the same power as God and is different from God, God is changed.

We may not think of generation from God as like an image. There is a great difference between the image and its model. The image is simply not a substance, not reality. (The Platonic nature of this objection does not need to be underlined.) The same arguments apply to the notion of generation as a character or impression.

Nor may we think of generation from God in terms of procession outwards. For if this were just on a single momentary occasion, what is the use of it? And if what comes out is good, why is God so niggardly in production? On the other hand, if there were more than one occasion, what was added after the first occasion? And in that case, is it being implied that God was incapable of achieving perfection at one stroke? It might, however, be argued that generation from God should be thought of not in terms of procession outwards but simply as activity, movement (*motus*). That there might be activity or movement which is within God, immanent in him, Candidus concedes, but that is not generation; and if there is movement towards the exterior, that is procession outwards, which is subject to all the objections which have just been raised.

But generation might be thought of as a form of overflow from God. This, says Candidus, is to think of God as a spring or fountain, and the image is open to the same sort of criticism that has been given before. Does the overflow remain in the spring? Obviously not. If we make the necessary adjustments then for God, we mean to say that there will be new angels and new worlds; but also that there will be no emptying of the original source. And that means doubling the difficulty about the unchangeable nature of God; because he will have to remain unchanged in spite of perpetual outflow from him, and also unchanged in spite of perpetual replenishment of the outflow. Again, other people say that generation comes about in accordance with the will and the act of God. But this and the final possibility (that generation is to be thought of in terms of a *typus*) we may ignore here, interesting though they are as questions in their own right.

Victorinus replied to this letter, as we have seen, but he makes no satisfactory answer to the questions raised and he continues to use the images questioned elsewhere. He emphasises (*AA* I 27, 23f) that '*est proprium eius quod primum est esse, quiescere*': 'it's the property of the first being to be at rest', but, somewhat on the lines of Plato, he is so overwhelmed by the notion of the mystery of God that he feels no language can do it justice. We saw that Plato in the *Sophist* confronted himself with the question of how we could possibly leave out life from our notion of the perfect: in the same way, in what seems to be a reminiscence of *Sophist* 248E, earlier on in the work I have just quoted, Victorinus says of the supreme beings 'without movement, that is, without action, what life or what intelligence is there?' (*AA* I 4, 4f) That he is not happy with attempts to reconcile traditional philosophical notions of the immutability of the first principle and what would seem to be required by scriptural pictures of God's activity in the universe is obvious from chapters 33 and 34 of the same work. He labours the problem sufficiently there to excuse us from doing it further: he eventually has to settle for a paradox that Augustine will return to: 'The Father is, by predominance, life in principle, having hidden inside him a movement which is at rest and moves witnin'. (*AA* I 42, 23ff)[3] (But of course both Victorinus and Augustine could call on Plotinus, where the fullness of being is 'at the same time, same and different, movement and rest, mobile and immobile'. (*Enn* V. 9. 10)

So far we have seen Victorinus continuing the Platonic tradition in regard both to the utter transcendence of God and just now in regard to the immutability, with its attendant difficulties. The transcendence of the unchanging perfection raises another traditionally associated problem, that of our knowledge of God. As might be expected from what we have seen so far, he lays heavy emphasis on two of the recognised ways to God, the way of negation and the way of eminence or transcendence. Discussions occur generally in the context of the Trinity, but if we again leave Trinitarian thought to one side we shall see enough of inherited material to convince us that Victorinus was still very much in the Platonic mould. He talks (*AA* I 49,11ff) of the One which is before all existence and before being itself, the One which is without existence and before being itself, the One which is without existence, without substance and without intelligence, because it is above all these, without form and lacking all forms. Then (26ff) he moves on to the transcendence of the One, which is described as more mobile than movement itself and more stable than rest itself.[4] All this is summed up at the beginning of the next chapter, 50, in the words: 'This is God, this is the father, pre-existing pre-intelligence and pre-existence, preserving his own blessedness and himself in an unmoving motion, and because of this, not needing others, perfect above the perfect … existing everywhere and nowhere.' Just before Victorinus describes God as existing everywhere and nowhere, he describes him as 'remaining in himself, alone in himself alone'. This brings us back to the old problem of how there can be contact between a God so utterly transcendent and the world. Victorinus, like Platonists before him, is quite prepared for syncretism when it suits him. So we find him saying (*AA* IV 18, 53ff): 'God is the primary existence, who lives necessarily and thinks himself. It is because the primary existence thinks itself that it thinks all things'. And again: 'If God is thinking or thought, when God thinks, he thinks himself'. (*AA* IV 27, 5ff) This is obviously recalling Book Lambda of the *Metaphysics* of Aristotle, even though Plotinus, for instance, would not have been happy with this picture of the supreme One. But Victorinus would not have shared the scruples of Plotinus, any more than he shared the scruples of Plato in the *Parmenides* about thinking of the Forms as thoughts of God: such certainly seems to be the import of *AA* IV 5, 24 ff.

In fact, however, Victorinus is prepared for a much more drastic answer to the question of our knowledge of God. He states it quite bluntly in *AA* III 6, 2ff: 'It is difficult to have a conception of God, but the aspiration is not entirely desperate'. He then gives his reasons for this statement. Firstly, God made the world so that through his divine works we might come to know him. Secondly, his *Logos*, his Son, his image and form, has opened a way of knowledge to him. Thirdly, God has breathed a soul into us and from that there is a part which is supreme in us, and so we touch God by that part by which we are from God and depend on him. Finally, we have received from God the Saviour and the Holy Spirit.

With this obvious mixture of pagan thought and Christian belief we may leave Victorinus. The first and third reasons have recurred frequently in earlier pagan theology and will recur later in Christian theology. We shall see that Augustine will take up both. That does not mean that he takes them from Victorinus: the third reason, for instance, on the soul, seems to be taken almost word for word by Victorinus from Plotinus. (V. I.I I) But Victorinus did open the way for Augustine to his God in a very practical fashion, and it is fitting that we should turn to Augustine next.

There is of course no implication intended that it was solely through Victorinus that Augustine came to his notion of God. He tells us in the Confessions (3, 4) that he had drunk in with his mother's milk the name of the Saviour, and it is obvious from his writings that he had never entirely shaken off the Christian beliefs that his mother tried so hard to implant and develop within him. But it was through the writings of the 'Platonists' especially that he had come to his mature notion of God, and it is with this that we are particularly concerned. At a later stage he was to write: 'None of them (the philosophers) have come closer to us (Christians) than these (the Platonists)'. (*CD* 8,5) 'Change a few words and propositions and they might be Christians'. (*VR* 4, 7) 'They are great men and almost divine'. (*O* 2,10, 28) In order to understand why he came to this position, we have to examine his life and character in more detail than we have done with any individual so far mentioned.

It is in Book Seven of the *Confessions* that Augustine begins his extended account of his discovery of the 'books of the Platonists'. He tells us a little later (8, 2) how he went along to Simplicianus and 'told him that I had read certain books of the Platonists which had been translated into Latin by Victorinus, one time professor of Rhetoric in Rome, who had, so I heard, died a Christian', and

Simplicianus congratulated him on his good fortune with these philosophers, for 'in the Platonists God and his Word are everywhere implied'. Agustine, apparently, had to read these works in translation, for he has told us earlier in the *Confessions* how as a boy he hated Greek, and it is generally assumed that he never became sufficiently competent in it to read it easily, or certainly that he could not do so at the time of his conversion. This was a pity, particularly since Augustine was keenly interested in philosophy. His weakness in Greek meant that his knowledge of philosophy was confined to what was available in Latin translation or in summarised form in handbooks.

Augustine, in fact, never did a proper 'course' in philosophy. His own description of his mental wanderings and enthusiasm is a sufficient indication of the untrained philosophical mind. The fact that the *Hortensius* of Cicero, at best a second-hand version of an exhortation to the life of philosophy, made such an impression on the 18-year-old Augustine shows us that at this stage in his development his mind was still philosophically uncritical. (*Conf.* 3, 4) He is proud of the fact that when he was barely twenty years old he 'read and understood, alone and unaided, the book of Aristotle's Ten Categories'. (*Conf.* 4,16) He says that the book 'came into my hands': he was not directed to it, any more than he was directed to even the *Hortensius*, which he had come across 'in the ordinary course of study'. He seems to have thought that the *Hortensius* was an original composition by Cicero; and the thing that pleased him most of all in Cicero's book was that it contained an exhortation 'not to this or that philosophical school, but wisdom itself, whatever it might be'. (*Conf.* 3, 4)

We might, then, expect, and we do find, in Augustine's writings, philosophical eclecticism. But his autobiography makes clear that Platonism was the philosophy which he had been born for. Long before he discovered 'the books of the Platonists', Augustine had been driven by the *eros* or desire for wisdom that we associate with Platonism. The *Hortensius* merely altered the direction of this drive: 'it gave me a new purpose and ambition. Suddenly all the vanity I had hoped in I saw as worthless, and with an incredible intensity of desire I longed after immortal wisdom' (3, 4) But the drive itself was already there: when he came to Carthage at the age of sixteen he says, 'I was not yet in love, but I was in love with love ... I sought some object to love, since I was thus in love with loving ... For within I was hungry, all for the want of that spiritual food which is thyself, my God ... My longing then was to love and to be loved, but most when I obtained the enjoyment of the body of the person who loved me'. (*Conf.* 3, 1) He was always a passionate man: what he says of himself in the *Confessions* could have been his motto: 'My love is my driving force'.

No passage in the *Confessions* is more revealing of the innate Platonism in Augustine's character than that in Book Four concerning the death of a friend. This happened when Augustine was about twenty two, in the year 376, when he had returned from Carthage to teach in his home town. They had known each other since childhood, but had become close friends only at this time, and his friend died suddenly when he had completed scarcely a year in a friendship that had 'grown sweeter to me than all the sweetness of the life I knew'. (*Conf.* 4, 4) What made the death even more heartbreaking was the fact that they had quarrelled most unexpectedly over a religious question at their last meeting and never had a chance to make it up. 'My heart was black with grief. Whatever I looked upon had the air of death. My native place was a prison house and my home a strange unhappiness. The things we had done together became sheer torment without him. My eyes were restless looking for him, but he was not there. I hated all places because he was not in them. They could not say "He will soon come", as they would in his life when he was absent. I became a great enigma to myself'. (*Conf.* 4, 4)

'I was filled with the thought that death might snatch away any man as suddenly as it had snatched him'. (*Conf.* 4, 6) For Augustine this was the experience which had most affected him so far in his life. 'Time', as he says, 'takes no holiday. It does not roll idly by, but through our senses works its own wonders in the mind'. (*Conf.* 4, 3) He gradually recovered from his grief but he never could forget the wound. In the *Confessions*, which were written about twenty years after this experience, the memory of it starts him on a long series of reflections on the relief one gets from tears, on human friendship, and on the transitoriness of all things set against the undying beauty of God. 'Wherever the soul of man turns, unless towards God, it cleaves to sorrow, even though the things outside God and outside itself to which it cleaves may be things of beauty. For these lovely things would be nothing at all unless they were from him. They rise and set: in their rising they begin to be, and they grow towards perfection, and once come to perfection they grow old, and they die: not all grow old but all die. Therefore when they rise and tend toward being, the more haste they make toward fullness of beings the more haste they make towards ceasing to be. That is their law'. (*Conf.* 4, 10)

The Platonic influence on this last passage is obvious, but it would be perverse to maintain that Augustine adopted such an attitude simply because he had read about it in the 'Platonists'. Neoplatonism was congenial to him because of the temperament he was born with. The ever-recurring turning outwards from the centre was something he had experienced in his own person and not just something he had read about in a book. What is probably the best-known quotation from Augustine is: 'Thou hast made us for thyself, O Lord, and our hearts are restless until they rest in thee'. (*Conf.* 1,1) His restlessness was not easily overcome, and the peace, security and certainty which he so longed for was not easily won. His was not a mind which relaxed easily in dogmatic slumbers, and it is obvious that one of his opponents went very near the bone when, as Augustine explains indignantly, 'He said that I (a bishop!) had the damnable mentality of a Carneades of the Sceptical Academy'. (*Contra litt. Petil.* 3, 21, 24)

This stung, because Augustine had been born with a sceptical mind which would not let him rest content until the combination of Neoplatonism and Christianity brought him to some sort of stability in 386. As Brown reminds us (p 49), 'his hero was Doubting Thomas'. Plato had put into the mouth of Socrates in the *Apology*, 'The life lived without questioning is not worth human living.' Agustine had not necessarily read that, but he lived by it, and it was part of the reason why the Sceptical Academy had in fact appealed so much to him as he searched for some philosophy to live by. For the *Hortensius* had filled him with an 'incredible intensity of desire for the immortal wisdom', but it had not told him where to look. It seems almost incredible to us that this exhortation to philosophy should make him look first to the scriptures. Here he was put off by the 'lowness' of their style, and then he turned to Manichaeism. Of this he was an excited apostle for a number of years, but here again he naturally had questions. When he presented these difficulties to the local Manichaeans he was fobbed off with the answer, 'Faustus will explain all that to you'. But Faustus, the much admired Manichaean intellectual in Africa, did not explain everything to Augustine when they eventually did meet. His faith in Manichaeism never recovered from this disappointment, and even though he stayed with Manichaean friends when he went to Rome in 383, 'the notion began to grow in me that the philosophers whom they call Academics were wiser than the rest, because they held that everything should be treated as a matter of doubt and affirmed that no truth can be understood by men'.

Yet he craved for certainty and he could not rest content with mere scepticism. He was, however, by nature incapable of simply accepting a body of belief that was handed over to him or, worse, imposed on him. As he said *after* his conversion, 'I am so constituted that I impatiently desire to apprehend truth not by belief alone but by understanding'. (*C. Acad.* 3, 20, 43) He was converted to Christianity through Platonism, but his early writings show us a mind in action that is more a parallel to the Platonic method than a result of it. We have no evidence, and it is highly unlikely, that Augustine read the early Socratic dialogues, yet his early writings contain an exposition of the Socratic procedure which Socrates himself might have envied: there is first the application of the negative *elenchos* or testing to clear away any unreliable beliefs or views that have been accepted uncritically, and then Augustine builds up his positive system.

Truth does exist, despite what the Sceptics say. If a man looks within himself he will see that no matter what else he doubts, it is certain that he is doubting. This is true and he is certain of this truth. (*VR* 73, 204-206) If truth and certainty exist anywhere there is a possibility that they may be extended. We know that we are, and are alive, and that we think. (*LA* 2, 3, 7; *BV*, 2 ,7; Sol. 2, 1, 1) We can be certain also of the truths of mathematics. (v. *C. Acad.* 3,11, 25; 0 2, 19, 50) As he said in *Conf.* 6, 4: 'I wanted to be as certain of things unseen as that seven and three make ten. For I had not reached the point of madness which denies that even this can be known; but I wanted to know other things as clearly as this, either such material things as were not present to my senses, or spiritual things which I did not know how to ahieve except corporeally'.

And so we arrive eventually at God, who is the fountain and source of all truth. (*O.* 2, 19, 51; *Mus.* 6, 12, 34) The argument is the Platonic one which we saw in the *Alcibiades* that by knowing oneself and one's soul truly, one comes to know God. Augustine was always fascinated by the mystery of personality, the movements of the will and the powers of the mind and memory. In Platonism he would have found the same awareness of the mystery of the unity of the human being, so torn in memories and desires (see the *Symposium*), and he would have had his own original views confirmed. At the very beginning of the *Soliloquies*, after his opening prayer, Augustine represents his reason as asking him to state in short form what he wants to know, and he answers, 'I want to know God and the soul'. Reason asks: 'Nothing more?' and Augustine replies: 'Nothing at all'. (*Sol.* 1, 7) 'I want to know myself, I want to know you'.

It is obvious that Augustine's path to God was not easy. He has described it for us in most detail in the *Confessions*, repeating briefer biographical accounts from the early works, and there is no dispute about the general outline at least of the story he tells. We have heard already of how the *Hortensius* set him on fire for wisdom, but this enthusiasm provided no answer to the three great problems which confronted him at the age of eighteen. These were the problems of evil, the problem of God and spirit, and the complex of problems arising from stories in the Old Testament. (*Conf.* 3, 7) He found no satisfactory answers to these problems for another thirteen years and then he was helped towards the answers by one man, St Ambrose, in Milan.

Augustine had given up teaching rhetoric in Carthage because of the rowdiness of his students there. He then went to Rome, in 383, at the age of twenty nine, but stayed only a year there before moving on to Milan. There he used to go along to hear Ambrose preaching, but not, he says, because of the content, but merely as a connoisseur would go to hear a great artist perform. Yet he could not help but be impressed by the content of what he heard. It was because of Ambrose that the problems connected with the Old Testament were dissolved for him: with these we do not need to concern ourselves. More important is the fact that it was through Ambrose that he began to see an answer to his more fundamental difficulties about God and evil.

Through Ambrose I say, because in fact it was Neoplatonism which was providing the answers which Augustine sought, and Ambrose can be taken as the most impressive representative of Christian Neoplatonism in Milan. Courcelle has tried to show that Ambrose drew on Plotinus in his sermons *De Isaac* and *De Bono mortis* and that Augustine heard these. (The fundamental theme of *De Isaac* is that evil is a privation of good.) Whatever about the details of this theory, there is no doubt that Ambrose and Neoplatonism played a large part in Augustine's conversion.[5] Some years before this, in 373, in the interval between Ambrose's call to be bishop and his baptism, Ambrose had been instructed by the priest Simplicianus, a close friend of Marius Victorinus who had not only written what we saw in the first part of this chapter, but had made translations into Latin from the Greek of Plotinus and Porphyry.

Courcelle (op cit pp 154 ff) argues that Augustine, very taken by Ambrose's teaching on man's spiritual likeness to God, through the mind or *nous*, discovered it was Plotinian. He wanted to be instructed by Ambrose, but Ambrose was too busy and sent him to

Theodorus, the expert on Plotinus in Milan. Augustine could not read the *Enneads* in Greek, and got from Theodorus a Latin translation of Plotinus by Victorinus. Apart from this formal study we should not forget how much Augustine would have learned from conversations in the atmosphere of Milan, and from listening to the memories of other people who had been swept off their feet, like him, by Neoplatonism. In particular, the priest Simplicianus played a very important part in his conversion, and he met him only after hearing Ambrose and reading some of the books of the Platonists.

According to Augustine, he read in these books what one could read in the gospel of St John, except that there was no mention of the Incarnation and the Redemption, and 'being admonished by all this to return to myself, I entered into my own depths, with you as guide'. (*Conf.* 7, 9 and 10) Now he learnt 'that god is a spirit, having no parts extended in length and breadth, to whose being bulk does not belong'. (*Conf.* 3, 7) In Book Ten of the *Confessions* (a book which was probably added to the completed structure), he looks back on this time of discovery and shows how the convictions then won have stayed with him. Chapters 6-27 of this book talk about his search for God, and chapters 27 to the end tell how God has now touched him and what are the results. To say that we have here reproduced the Middle Platonic three ways might give the impression that Augustine was another pedestrian scholastic. It is necessary to read only a few chapters of the *Confessions* to see how false that impression would be. But there is no doubt that time and again in his discussion of God traditional pagan motifs reappear, even if not transmuted by his own very personal style. Chapter six of Book Ten starts by saying: 'It is with no doubtful knowledge, Lord, but with utter certainty that I love you'. And he explains why, with a combination of St Paul and one of the oldest and most popular pagan arguments for the existence of God. 'And indeed heaven and earth and all that is in them tell me wherever I look that I should love you, and they cease not to tell it to all men, so that there is no excuse for them'. Then he asks what is God and the answer begins on the ways of negation and eminence. 'But what is it that I love when I love you?' and the first answer is of the beauty of any bodily thing, and so on. 'None of these things do I love in loving my God'. But then there follows: 'Yet in a sense I do love light and melody and fragrance and food and embrace when I love my God' – but in a form far superior to anything experienced in this world.

Then begins the description of the ascent to God, a way of approach that had not lost its attractiveness since Plato's *Symposium*. 'And what is this God? I asked the earth and it answered "I am not he".' I asked the sea and the deeps and the creeping things ... the heavens, the sun, the moon, the stars. And they answered "We are not your God; seek higher". And I said to all the things that throng about the gateway of the senses: "Tell me of my God, since you are not he. Tell me something of him". And they cried out in a great voice: "He made us". My question was my gazing upon them, and their answer was their beauty. And I turned to myself and said: "And you, who are you?', and I answered: "A man".' Augustine goes on to say that a man is body and soul. By the body he had already sought God, 'but the interior art is the better', because it knows, through the senses. 'I the inner man knew them, I, I the soul, through the senses of the body'. Reason marks man off from the animals, but reason demonstrates man's superiority only when it judges the world, and is not merely a recipient, subject to the world.

Whatever, then, God is, he is superior to the highest thing in the world, and that is the topmost point of the soul. Therefore, 'by that same soul I shall ascend to Him'. (*Conf.* 10, 7) 'And so I come to the fields and vast palaces of memory' (*Conf*.1 0, 8), and Augustine then describes the extraordinary things the mind can do because of memory, and in doing so returns to the puzzle that has always fascinated him, the unity of personality and personal identity. 'And in my memory too I meet myself – I recall myself, what I have done, when and where and in what state of mind I was when I did it' ... 'In fact I cannot totally grasp all that I am. Thus the mind is not large enough to contain itself ... How can it not contain itself? As this question struck me, I was overcome with wonder and almost stupor. We are men going afar to marvel at the heights of mountains, the mighty waves of the sea, the long courses of great rivers, the vastness of the ocean, the movements of the stars, yet leaving themselves unnoticed'.

Augustine then turns to questions which the mind can deal with and which can yet be scarcely thought of as memory images: questions such as 'whether a thing is, what it is, of what sort it is'. They did not come through the senses, he says. 'Very well then, whence and how did they get into my memory? I do not know. For when I first learned them I was not relying on some other man's mind, but recognised them in my own; and I saw them as true and committed them to my mind as if placing them where I could get at them again whenever I desired. Thus they must have been in my mind even before I learned them, though they were not in my memory'. (*Conf.* 10, 10)

This is obviously reminiscent of Plato's doctrine of recollection, even though Augustine does not mention Plato here (and he is not averse to drawing on other philosophies when it suits him). All that follows is also essentially Platonic, with its emphasis on the independence of the mind, for 'the mind and the memory are not two separate things'. (*Conf.* 10,14) 'Great is the power of memory, a thing, O my God, to be in awe of, a profound and immeasurable multiplicity; and this thing is my mind, this thing am I'. But Augustine, of course, is not interested in dwelling on himself. 'I shall pass beyond memory to find you, O truly good and certain loveliness' (although, typically, Augustine immediately raises a paradox: 'If I find you beyond my memory, then shall I be without memory of you? And how shall I find you if I am without memory of you?'). He says that in seeking in and beyond memory it is happiness he is seeking, and 'happiness is known to all, and if they could be asked with one voice whether they wish for happiness, there is no doubt whatever that they would all answer yes. And this could not be unless the thing itself, signified by the word, lay somehow in the memory'. (*Conf.* 10, 21)

But how does it lie in the memory? 'Happiness is not to be seen by the eye because it is not a body'. 'But where and when had I any experience of happiness, that I should remember it and love it and long for it?' (*Conf.* 10, 21) Yet everyone does find some joy in his memory and recognises it when he hears the word happiness. Men wish to have their joy in the truth: they therefore love the truth, but allow themselves to be distracted from it because of what seem to them more pressing concerns. So the mind allows itself to be deceived and it changes, but the God of the mind remains unchangeable over all. (*Conf.* 10, 25) 'Where then did I find you to learn of you, save in yourself, above myself? Place there is none, we go this way and that, and place there is none. You, who are Truth, reside everywhere to answer all who ask counsel of you'. And Augustine's search ends with the words: 'Late have I loved you, O beauty so ancient and so new; late have I loved you. For you were within me, and I outside; and I sought you outside and in my unloveliness fell upon these lovely things that you have made'. (*Conf.*10, 27)

Augustine has found God by looking within himself, which yet also means going far beyond himself. We see once again the recurrence of the old transcendence versus immanence problem, but this is the first appearance in such a highly personal shape. I have so far emphasised the personal aspect of Augustine's thought, and have tended to talk of parallels in Augustine to the Platonic

way of thinking rather than the influence on Augustine of Platonism. But we have Augustine's own explicit statement on how
great was the help that the books of the Platonists provided for
him, and the combination of his temperament and his reading at
this crucial period meant that the influence on Christian thinking
on God that came from him was largely Platonic in inspiration.
What is important for us is not to distinguish the personal and the
Platonic in his thought but to highlight the Platonism that was
passed on through him. This should also help to redress the im-
balance that might have come from excessive emphasis on the
personal contribution of Augustine. For even in what might appear the most personal passages there is often a Platonic background. The *Confessions* for instance is cast in the form of a prayer
to God, and we might take this to be the natural mode of expression of the Christian bishop which Augustine was when he wrote
it. And yet for a contemporary, as Peter Brown points out, 'at first
sight, it was easy to place the *Confessions*: they were patently the
work of a Neo-Platonic philosopher. They were, for instance,
written in the form of a prayer to God that was common to a long
tradition of religious philosophy. For the God of the Platonists
was an Unknown God, so far above the human mind that the philosopher could only increase his knowledge of him by committing himself entirely to him. Philosophical enquiry, therefore,
verged on the concentrated quality of an act of prayer ... Prayer ...
was a recognised vehicle for speculative enquiry'. (op cit pp 165f)

The first five chapters of Book One are taken up with direct
prayer to God and reflections on what prayer implies. Prayer is an
indication of the mystery of the relationship between man and
God, both mysteries in themselves; and when Augustine talks of
the mystery of God in chapter four of Book One he uses the language of paradox which had been consecrated now by hundreds of
years of philosophical usage. 'What then are you, my God? ...
You are fixed there, yet incomprehensible, unchanging, yet
changing everything, never new and never old, but making all
things new ... always in action and yet always at rest ... You
change the things you make yet you never change your mind'.
And yet all this talk reveals only the insufficiency of language.
'Yet with all this, what have I said my God? Or what does anyone
say when he talks of you? ... Even those who say most are dumb'.
(l, 4)

Augustine was not, of course, thinking of Proclus when he
wrote this, but he is fitting into the same Platonic mould. Equally
Platonic are the meditations which convinced him that God exists
and which are fairly certainly based on his reading of 'the books

of the Platonists'.[6] 'I asked myself how it was that I could appreciate the beauty of material bodies ... and what it was that enabled me to make correct judgements about things that are subject to change and to rule that one thing should be like this and another should not be like that. I wondered how it was that I was able to judge them in this way, and I realised that above my own mind which was liable to change, there was the never changing true eternity of truth ... The power of reason, realising that in me, too, it was liable to change, led me to consider the source of its own understanding. It withdrew my thoughts from their normal course ... so that it might discover what light it was that had been shed upon it when it proclaimed for certain that what was immutable was better than that which was not and how it had come to know the immutable itself. For unless by some means it had known the immutable, it could not possibly have been certain that it was preferable to the mutable. And so, in an instant of awe, my mind attained to the sight of That Which Is'. (*Conf.* 7, 17)

This may be drawn directly from Plotinus, but ultimately it goes back to Plato and his various efforts to establish the theory of Forms. The ascent to the unchanging Truth and Beauty which is God is effected for Augustine by means of the soul. The soul and the mind belong to the realm of the divine and the immaterial, removed from all corporeal corruption. It is this Platonic motif which Augustine picks out (in *De Beata Vita* 1, 4) as the one which impressed him most as he struggled in Milan to achieve some certainty. 'I noticed how frequently the point was emphasised in the talks of our priest (probably Ambrose) and occasionally in your own (Theodorus) that when we thought about God, we should not think about anything corporeal, nor when we thought about the soul, for that is the one thing in the world nearest to God'. He goes on to tell Theodorus that he is obsessed with the problem of the soul at this time (385), and it is obvious even from the titles of his books over the next few years that he remained obsessed with it. The body-soul dualism which is such a prominent part of Plato's philosophy owes its perpetuation in Western thought more perhaps to Augustine than to any other person.

There was a considerable emphasis in Plato on the notion that the process of becoming like unto God involved the flight of the soul from the body and evil. But Augustine did not of course have to turn to Platonism to discover the problem of evil, even though he did find the beginnings of a solution in Neoplatonism. He tells us that the question of why we do evil was one that struck him when he was still quite young, and one should not be accused of undue psychologising for drawing attention to the possible influence of Monica here as well. 'Why is it that we do evil?', he writes in 388. 'You are asking the very question which terribly troubled me when I was still very much a youth and which drove me when I tired of trying to answer it into the arms of the heretics'. (*LA* 1, 2, 4) These heretics were the Manichaeans whom he tells us he turned to when his 'incredible desire for wisdom', stimulated by Cicero's *Hortensius*, was not satisfied by his reading of the scriptures. We have referred already to the three great questions which faced him at this stage and which Ambrose was to help to provide answers for: the Old Testament problem, the question of God which we have just discussed, and the first one which he mentions in *Confessions* 3, 7, the problem of evil. 'I did not know the other reality which truly is, and through my own stupid cleverness I allowed myself to be taken in by fools who deceived me with such questions as: Whence comes evil? And is God bounded by a bodily shape and has he hair and nails?' He then gives the answer which he later found to the problem of evil. 'I did not know that evil has no being of its own but is only an absence of good, so that it simply is not'. But this was the answer which he found in Milan. Before that, when he went to Rome in 383, he tells us that even though he was then losing faith in Manichaeism he still stayed with the Manichees, because he still was bothered about the notion of God, and 'I still held the view that it was not we that sinned, but some other nature sinning in us; and it pleased my pride to be beyond fault'. (*Conf.* 5, 10) He found it difficult to think of God as anything other than body, and 'I thought that the substance of evil was in some sense similar, and had its own hideous and formless bulk. And because such poor piety as I had constrained me to hold that the good God could not have created any nature evil, I supposed that there were two opposing powers, each infinite, yet the evil one lesser and the good one greater'.

He continued to wrestle with the problem as the influence of Ambrose in Milan grew stronger over him and the influences of Manichaeism weakened. 'I set myself to examine an idea I had heard, namely that our free-will is the cause of our doing evil, and your just judgement the cause of our suffering evil'. (Conf. 7, 3)[7] The one clear advance that this reflection helped him to make was that 'I was quite certain that it was myself and no other who willed, and I came to see that the cause of my sin lay there'. But he was still well aware that he had not got to the root of the matter, even though 'I could not draw the conclusion that unless you were incorruptible there was something better than my God'.

(*Conf.* 7, 4) He had to discover the books of the Platonists before he could get further light. The Neoplatonists helped him to argue that 'all things that are corrupted are deprived of some goodness'. It is obvious that many things are corrupted. 'But if they were deprived of all goodness, they would be totally without being ... If they were deprived of all goodness, they would be altogether nothing: therefore as long as they are, they are good. Thus whatsoever things are, are good; and that evil whose origin I sought is not a substance (existing in its own right), because if it were a substance existing in its own right it would be good ... Thus, I saw clearly and realised that you have made all things good, and that there are no substances not made by you'. (*Conf.* 7, 12) So Augustine is forced to the conclusion: 'To you, then, evil utterly is not – and not only to you, but to your whole creation likewise, evil is not'. This is a remarkable conclusion in view of the central role played by the problem of evil in his thought up to now. If evil has no real separate existence, as the Neoplatonists say, why do we talk about evil at all? Augustine reproduces the Neoplatonic 'aesthetic' reasoning, that a variety and therefore a lack of sameness, even of goodness, is necessary for an overall satisfactory effect. 'In certain of the parts of creation there are some things which pass for evil because they do not harmonise with other things; yet these same things do harmonise with still others and thus are good; and in themselves they are good'. (*Conf.* 7, 13) 'My own experience had shown me that there was nothing extraordinary in the same bread being loathsome to a sick palate and agreeable to a healthy, and in light being painful to sore eyes which is a joy to clear. Your justice displeases the wicked: but so do the viper and the smaller worms: yet these you have created good, and suited to the lowler parts of your creation to which lower parts, indeed the wicked themselves, are well suited, insofar as they are unlike you, though they become suited to the higher parts as they grow more like you. So that when I now asked what is iniquity, I realised that it was not a substance but a swerving of the will which is turned towards lower things and away from you, O God, who are the supreme substance: so that it casts away what is most inward to it and swells greedily for outward things'. (*Conf.* 7, 17)

It was to be expected that Augustine could not accept this answer to the problem of evil (intellectually satisfactory though it might be) with the serenity of Plotinus who had proposed it. The difficulty which the problem of the will caused him is clear from the description which follows of the struggles he went through on his way to moral conversion. (see especially *Conf.* 8, 9) But it would take us too far afield to consider even briefly Augustine's reflections on these matters which were derived from his reading in areas other than Greek philosophy. We must be content with noting that through him in particular the Neoplatonic solution passed into the Christian tradition, though that does not of course imply that all problems about evil were thereby removed for Christians. We shall see consideration of further aspects of it, especially in regard to freedom of the will, in more concise form in Boethius to whom we now turn.

Boethius (480-524) is still best known for his work *On the Consolation of Philosophy*, but whatever fame that work has nowadays is small compared to what it had for at least six centuries after his death. As Knowles says, '(his) influence upon the literature, the thought and the method of the eleventh and twelfth centuries, and indeed upon that of the great scholastics down to and including St Thomas, was second only to that of Augustine'.[8] Yet the *Consolation* was the last of his works, and could almost be described as accidental, and what he himself, if he had lived, would probably have regarded as a parergon. Because he had decided, while still relatively young, to translate into Latin and explain or comment on all the works of Plato and Aristotle. This project, which he was eminently well equipped to carry through, was barely started when he was executed in 524. He was born of a prominent family in Rome about 480 AD. His father had been consul and he himself became consul in 510, although the real ruler was King Theodoric the Ostrogoth. But Theodoric obviously thought highly of him and his career increased in brilliance until Theodoric became suspicious of him and he was put on trial and imprisoned. Boethius protests his innocence in the *Consolation* which he wrote while in prison, but the forthrightness of his language seems to indicate that he knew his chances of ultimate acquittal were slight. He was executed after a year, in 524 or 525.

His translation project had by this time only begun. He had translated the greater part of the *Organon* of Aristotle, and we shall see his indebtedness to the *De Interpretatione* in particular which he commented on. Another very important work was his translation and commentary on Porphyry's *Introduction*. Apart from that we have some short theological treatises, with particular emphasis on the Trinity, where his knowledge and application of Greek philosophy and its terminology were to prove of lasting importance. He was obviously a professed Christian, but the *Consolation* is so studiously philosophical in the traditional sense that it has caused doubts as to whether or not Boethius was a believing

Christian in the last year of his life when he wrote the book. I think that doubts about Boethius' Christianity are unjustified: Boethius is writing as a philosopher in the *Consolation*, as Augustine had been, very largely, in his early writings, but in neither case have we a rejection of, or aversion from, Christian theology. In Boethius' case we need not see any more than the natural desire to show that even unaided reason can justify God's ways to man, and, implicity, the wish to demonstrate that there is no inconsistency between (Greek) philosophy and Christian theology.

In any case, the *Consolation* had a very great influence on the succeeding Christian centuries, as Courcelle in particular has shown. As we read through the work we can see the recurrence of traditional pagan motifs about God which Boethius, like Augustine, passed on to the Christians. As Knowles again says, Boethius 'put into currency ideas and formulae on eternal life, on the reconciliation of God's foreknowledge with man's freewill, on the purely negative character of evil, and on the true freedom and beatitude of the just man unjustly condoned to suffer, which have ever since become part of the Christian heritage'. (op cit p 54) The question of the existence of God did not bother Boethius any more than it did his pagan predecessors whom we have examined: with him, as with them, the problem is how to discern God. In his plight, as might be expected, it is the question of the existence of evil which forces itself upon his attention, and how, if we accept the providence of a good and all-knowing God, men can be free to do, or suffer, good and evil. It is not surprising that Boethius, in facing these problems, shows the influence of most of the philosophical schools, given the extraordinary width and depth of his philosophical reading. But the Neoplatonic influence is predominant: and on the question of God, Courcelle goes as far as to say that his thought is much more impregnated with Neoplatonism that that of Augustine.[9]

Boethius follows the Platonic tradition in talking of God as good or the good. Men seek after happiness and through their beatitude they become like God, or as he says, once again continuing an old tradition, 'it is fitting that the blessed are gods'. (*CP* IV Pr. 3, 28f) Each day, he says, the lady Philosophy impressed upon him that maxim of Pythagoras 'Follow God', shaping him so that he might become like God. (*I* Pr. 4, 141ff) .His reflection on happiness and the good confirm him in his belief in the supreme good which is God. 'The supreme good contains all that is good within it and if anything were missing to it it could not be the supreme good, because something would remain outside it which could be wished for'. (*III Pr.* 2, 7ff) The very existence of imperfection is a proof of the existence of perfection. Things could not come into being unless there were some perfect source. The consensus of the human race is that God, the first of all things, is good. 'And since nothing can be thought of which is better than God, who could doubt that that than which there is nothing better is good?' 'Therefore so that our reasoning might not go on to infinity, we must confess that the supreme God is filled with supreme and perfect goodness'. His goodness comes from himself: he cannot be dependent on, and therefore inferior to, something else. Nor can there be two supreme goods, because if they differ one must be missing something which the other has got. So, he says, 'we have shown that blessedness and God are the supreme good'. The corollary that is drawn from this is reminiscent of both Plato's 'likening to God' and Aristotle's *Ethics*: 'As men are made just by the obtaining of justice and wise by the obtaining of wisdom, similarly those who obtain divinity must become gods. Therefore everyone that is blessed is a god, but by nature there is only one God; but there may be many by participation'. (*III Pr.* 10, 11-90)

Boethius also points to the order in the universe, in spite of all its diversity, as another indication of the control of One God who rules all things. 'He, himself remaining quiet, disposes and orders all the varieties of changes. This, whatever it is, by which things created continue as they are and are moved, I call God, a name which is used by all'. (*III Pr.* 12, 23ff) And Philosophy tells him that since he thinks like that, just a little effort will ensure that he will return to his fatherland in safety. This is obviously Neoplatonic language as is the whole description of the world process, the emergence from and the return to the One or the Good, God. All that exists is good. 'I have just told you', Philosophy says, 'that whatever exists is one, and that the one is good, and it follows from this that whatever exists must also be good'. (*IV Pr.* 3, 44ff) All things have had their beginning from God. (*I Pr.* 5, 27ff) 'It cannot be denied that there is something in existence which is, as it were, the foundation of all goodness'. (*III. Pr.* 10, 7ff) The famous poem nine of the third book of the *Consolation* not only summarises the first part of the book but goes back to the *Timaeus* for its explanation of the emergence of the world. God, we are told (line 4), was not moved to action by external causes, but as he is without jealousy or envy his goodness overflowed. As the Form of the highest good, he shaped the universe on the supreme model, and himself beautiful made it beautiful, ruling it by the power of his mind. (line 5ff) But although God has made this changing universe he is himself unchanging, '*stabilisque manens das cuncta move-ri*'. (line 3) It is his love that binds the universe together, and because of it all things seek to return to their source in him. They cannot persist unless they flow back to the cause which gave them being. Philosophy has already told him in the first book that it is because he has forgotten his source and his end that he is now plunged in such grief: he has forgotten that he is a man. (*I Pr*. 6, 33ff)

But if all that exists is good, if the universe is the creation of a good God, what is the source of evil? And why does the good man suffer? These are old questions by the time that Boethius is writing, but for him they are not just abstract philosophical problems which must be dealt with for the sake of the completeness of the system. His consolation depends on the answers he can find to these questions. And the answers are again in the Platonic tradition. Plato had insisted that man is responsible for his actions: morality depends on the possibility of freedom to do evil as well as good. Boethius is similarly concerned to show that we merit praise or blame for our actions. But if God is all-powerful and foresees all that will take place, and if his providence governs the world, how do we account for the existence of evil? Boethius has to deal with the problems of Providence and fate, God's foreknowledge and human free will.

Boethius is convinced that God is good and that everything that comes from him is good. God is also almighty, and there is nothing he cannot do. But the good God can do no evil, and therefore, Philosophy argues, evil is nothing. (*III Pr*. 12, 80) This neat argument is unfortunately at variance with the facts of experience, and Boethius replies to Philosophy at the beginning of book IV that one of the main reasons for his bewilderment and grief is that, when there is a good ruler of all things, there can be any evil at all or that it can pass unpunished. The evil prosper and the good suffer. Philosophy must therefore attempt to justify the ways of God to man.

She does so with the help of Plato's *Gorgias* and Aristotle's logic. Good and evil are contraries. All men desire to arrive at what they consider good. Good men by their very nature seek the highest good: there is nothing beyond. Men therefore who seek for something other than goodness are seeking non-being, for being means preserving the proper order of nature. If the wicked therefore can only do evil and evil has been agreed to be nothing, it is clear, says Philosophy, that the wicked can do nothing. And Boethius agrees that it is very clear. (*IV Pr*. 2) Philosophy goes on to argue in the next section that evil is denaturing: he who abandons virtue, since he cannot become a sharer in the divine condition, is turned into a beast. (IV *Pr.* 3, 67 ff) The evil are their own punishment, and so, Philosophy argues next, the wicked are happier being punished than if they escaped justice. Because whatever is just is good and so the wicked have some share in goodness when they are justly punished. (IV *Pr.* 4)

Boethius concedes that the logic of this seems impeccable, granted the premises, but is quite rightly sceptical about its appeal to common sense. (IV *Pr.* 4, 91ff) He still wants to know (IV *Pr.* 5) why things are turned upside down and the evil prosper. This is particularly difficult to understand when we believe in God and believe that he, and not simply chance, rules the world. It is this extraordinary fact, this *miraculum*, which troubles him most of all. (IV *Pr* .6, 4) And Philosophy concedes that this is the most difficult question of all and involves discussion of Providence, fate, chance, God's knowledge and predestination, and free will.

The distinction is first drawn between Providence and fate, once again in an obviously Neoplatonic fashion. Providence is the divine plan for the universe, seen as one unchanging system in the Divine Mind; fate is the unfolding of this plan in the world of space and time. So fate follows from Providence as the work of a craftsman follows from the unified design which he has in his mind, as the execution follows on the idea. The old image of the centre and the circle is used: Providence is like the unmoving centre point, and fate like the circle that revolves round it. The fixedness and reliability of the course of events and the law that governs them decreases as one moves out from the centre. This notion goes back not just to Plotinus, but to Plato on the 'purity' of mathematics and Aristotle's discussion of order and 'the division of the sciences' in the *Metaphysics*. And the Stoic notion of an unbreakable connection of causes is added to this mixture of sources: their conception of Providence tries to ensure that, amidst the flux of things, the unchanging *Logos* orders all for the best.

All these are, however, very general considerations. The question must still be asked, why is the good God impartial to evil people and good? The answers to this are once again traditional. Have human beings sufficient knowledge to judge properly who is good and who is evil? And can they really be sure of what will be good for some and bad for others? God alone knows this. How the good have endured suffering is sometimes an inspiration to others, and, even apart from that, the very sight of suffering and evil has forced some to amend their lives. Men also create so much revulsion that even people like them react against them and become good. (IV *Pr.* 6) Besides, evil gives the good an opportunity for increase of wisdom, as battle gives the soldier an opportunity for increase of glory. Our fortune is within our own control, and sufferings should be seen either as a means of exercising ourselves or as something that corrects or punishes us.

This seems to satisfy Boethius but it does seem to indicate that God's control is absolute. Why then do we talk of 'chance'? Philosophy insists that there cannot be any question of something coming from nothing. Providence governs all things, and chance is subjective in the sense that it is the unexpected outcome of a combination of causes, the result that follows on the unintended conjunction of processes, each of which was done for a specific purpose. 'My Aristotle' is referred to as the authority for such a position (V *Pr.* 1, 35ff), but the whole question of chance and that which follows, on free will, is one that had been much debated in Stoicism. Philosophy insists that there can be no reasonable nature unless it possesses free will. But there are varieties of freedom, and Philosophy talks in very Platonic fashion of how our minds can become slaves of our bodies. (V *Pr.* 2) It is emphasised by Philosophy that all this takes place in accordance with predestination and this emphasis confronts Boethius with a dilemma. How can God infallibly foresee all things, and yet this foresight co-exist with human free-will? God's dignity seems to demand the primacy of his knowledge: things will happen because God foresees them, and his knowledge must be certain and unwavering. 'Therefore there is no freedom in human plans or actions, since the divine mind, which foresees all things without error or mistake, ensures that these plans and actions will have only one outcome'. (V *Pr.* 3, 81ff)

Yet with such determinism there is no room for talk about morality. Besides if human action is predetermined by God, and some of it is, as we know, evil, does this mean that God is the cause of evil? Moreover, if everything is already fixed, there is no place left for prayer and there is no point in it. In order to avoid this unwelcome conclusion, Philosophy points out that just as our knowledge of events which are actually going on at the moment does not create for them any necessity to happen, so foreknowledge implies no necessity in future events. (V *Pr.* 4, 60ff) Besides, there are different kinds of knowledge even in human knowing. Now it is the general consensus that God is eternal, and his eternity obviously must be taken into consideration when we talk of his

knowledge. Eternity is described as the entire and perfect possession altogether of an endless life. This means that past and future,
as well as the now, are present to it. It is *sui compos* (V *Pr.* 6, 29), not
subject to or measured by anything else. Life as we know it is an
attempt at an imitation of God's eternal life, but it can only imitate
by moving, while God's life exists there perfectly in stability.
God's knowledge therefore is above all movement of time and remains simply ever present. All things both past and future, are
present to it and are going on in the way that we say things are going on just now. Yet when we see things go on, we do not make
them necessary: we are not responsible for causing them. So too
God sees all things in his eternal presence, whether they are what
we would regard as 'necessary' like the rising of the sun, or 'accidental', like the fact that a man is walking down a street. Even
though God sees things, which to men are future and depend on
free will, as present, the fact of his seeing them does not take away
from their freedom. And if action is free, morality is preserved.

Boethius ends the *Consolation* by saying that prayer, also, is
therefore a reasonable and praiseworthy activity. But he does not
argue the point and it is difficult to see how he could. His image of
God positioned high above the world and observing all the action
in it going on at the same time, and therefore not interfering in it
and spoiling free will, is appealing but intellectually does not remain satisfying. It pleases our imagination because of the illusion
of immobility that we have if we are watching people and objects
from a great height. But we do not claim to have providence for
such people; above all, we have not created what we see, whereas
God has created and set in order what he sees.

Yet the *Consolation* is a remarkable work, and the last book, particularly, which we have just considered, is an impressive piece of
argumentation. Courcelle has traced the immense influence it had
in the Middle Ages. This influence in regard to thinking on God
was fundementally Platonist and specifically Neoplatonist, like
that of the other two Christian thinkers we have discussed in this
chapter. Like them too he wrote works on specifically Christian
theology, dealing with questions concerning the Trinity and the
natures of Christ. Some points from these we have already seen in
connection with the *Consolation*. But in these works also we can
see the continuation and transmission of the old Platonic tradition,
with the emphasis of the unity of God (*De Trin.* 3, *C. Eutyschen* 4,
37), his superiority to ordinary substance (*De Trin.* 4), and his immutability. (*De Trin.* 2,15f; *C. Eutyshen* 2, 24f, 6, 10ff) Boethius never
achieved his ambition of transmitting all Plato and Aristotle to the

Latin world; but he transmitted enough, and above all he did it so beautifully, that he became through his philosophical work one of the fathers of Christian theology in the Middle Ages. What the effect would have been had he achieved his ambition of translating Plato and Aristotle into Latin remains one of the most fascinating unanswered questions in the history of thought.

CHAPTER EIGHT

Pseudo-Dionysius
and John Scotus Eriugena

Sheldon-Williams says of Eriugena: 'By translating the Pseudo-Dionysius he laid the foundations of Western Mysticism'.[1] Important though that was, it does not exhaust Eriugena's contribution of the history of the philosophy of religion. An indication of his importance is given in a remark of Wallis (op cit p 96) about Porphyry: 'It was Porphyry's version of Neoplatonism that dominated the Western tradition *until Eriugena's ninth-century translation of the Dionysian corpus'* (my italics). We shall see that through his translation he continued the main lines of Platonist speculation on the Divinity and transmitted it to Thomas Aquinas who had been the dominant figure in Western theology in general, and not just in mysticism. This speculation Eriugena took not only from the Greek: he continued the Latin tradition which he found particularly in Augustine, but also in Ambrose and Boethius. His work was not confined to translation: Sheldon-Williams continues the sentence quoted above by saying that 'his *Periphyseon* ... is the most impressive piece of philosophical writing between the ages of St Augustine and St Thomas'. But it was his ability to translate Greek which distinguished him in his time and which made him so important for the largely Greekless scholastic philosophy. Besides, even his original work is heavily influenced by his reading of the Greek fathers, especially Gregory of Nyssa, Maximus, and the mysterious Dionysius.

We approach the last named through Eriugena because we are concerned with influences, and Dionysius' influence was transmitted primarily through the Latin translations of Eriugena. So Dionysius became 'one of the main sources of mediaeval thought', as Gilson says.[2] About Dionysius we know practically nothing. Eriguena himself , and nearly everyone else until the fifteenth century, thought that he was who he said he was, the disciple of St Paul, and so he was called St Dionysius the Areopagite. This confusion gave his writings enormous prestige; they were, after all, practically apostolic. Consequently, as Knowles says, 'through a misapprehension without parallel in either sacred or profane lit-

erature, much of his teaching has become embedded in the theological tradition of the West.' (op cit p 56) For his works still retained their value in translation, of course. We can see that
whoever 'Dionysius' was, he had been subjected to the influence
of later Neoplatonic speculation. It has been concluded from this,
and from the silence of the Fathers of the first four centuries about
him, and for some other reasons, that the corpus could not have
been written before the end of the fifth century. [3]

We need not concern ourselves further with Dionysius' background. The writings that have come down to us are *The Divine
Names*, *The Celestial Hierarchy*, *The Ecclesiastical Hierarchy*, *Mystical
Theology*, and ten letters. These writings had been already translated into Latin in the 830s, but in 850 Charles the Bald asked Eriugena
to do a new translation, evidently because the first translation was
not satisfactory.[4] (Eriugena, referring to the first chapter of *The Divine Names*, says that Dionysius 'in his usual way expresses himself in an involved and distorted language, and therefore many
find him extremely obscure and difficult to understand' (*Peripyse-
on* 509c). In these works we find once again the chief themes of
Platonist speculation on the divinity.

God is the One, the giver of good and light which flows out on
us and draws us back to him. (*CH* c. l, *DN* c. l) 'Theology glorifies
the author of all as One ... One because all things through the outstanding nature of its single Oneness, and the cause of all things
not departing from its unity. For there is no being without a share
in the One ... Without the One there will be no multiplicity, but
the One can exist without multiplicity'. (*DN* c. 13, 1- 2) 'And you
will not find any of the things that are which is not in the One
(after which hyperessentially the whole Godhead is named), and
is what it is'. (DN c.13, 3) The One God is also good. 'God is by his
very being good, and as essential goodness, extends his goodness
into all things. And just as our sun, not through thinking or making choice, but by the very fact of its existence, gives light to all
things which are capable of sharing in their own way in its illumination, so the good (which is above the sun as the archetype by its
very existence is transcendently above the dull image) sends out
upon all things according to their measure the rays of its total
goodness ... (The intelligible and intellectual beings) have their
fixity from this goodness, and their foundation is from there, and
their continuity and preservation. From there they are fed on
good things. Through desiring this they have both their being and
their well-being; being conformed to this, as far as in them lies,
they become like the good, and pass on to those that are below

them the gifts that come from the good, as the divine command imposes'. (*DN* c.4, 1) The desire or yearning for the Good runs right through the universe and gives it its cohesion. 'True reasoning will dare to say that he who is responsible for all things loves all through the excess of his goodness, and through it he makes all things, perfects all things, continues all things in existence, and turns back all things towards himself. The Divine Love is the good yearning for the good for the sake of the good. This is the Love which brings about the good in the things that are, and being pre-existent to a superlative degree in the good, did not allow him to remain unproductive in himself, but rather moved him to act in accordance with the excellence of his powers for the production of all things'. (*DN* c.4, 10)

All this is not merely Platonist but could be said to be taken from Plato himself: central passages in the *Republic*, *Timaeus* and *Symposium* on the Sun, the creative good and the object of desire are alluded to, directly or indirectly, and the *Parmenides* might have been used for the One. It is also of course Neoplatonist. But to cite just this as typical of Dionysius would be to misrepresent him. For what is said here could be assigned to two of the three ways which were imposed on the 'theology' of Plato, the way of analogy and the way of eminence: more prominent in Dionysius, and the feature which promoted the remark of Sheldon-Wiilliams quoted at the start of this chapter, is the negative way, the way to mystical theology. God is so utterly beyond all: we can know or say that it is only negation which allows us to speak the truth. We talk about manifestations of God: what he is in himself is completely beyond our grasp. So at the beginning of chapter five of the *Divine Names*, when turning to talk about 'Being' as a name applied to God, Dionysius warns us that 'the purpose of this treatment is not to reveal the reality which is beyond reality, *qua* beyond Reality. For this is unutterable, and it is unknowable, and it is entirely beyond revealing, and even removes the meaning of unity'. At the beginning of the whole work he has warned us that, apart from what scripture tells us (itself requiring very careful interpretation), 'we must not dare to speak or to form any conception about the hyperessential and hidden Godhead'. Unknowing is best suited to the hyperessential: which is beyond languages mind and being, and it is in Unknowing that the hyperessential knowledge is to be sought. 'That One which is beyond reasoning is not to be examined by any form of reasoning, and that Good which is beyond words is not to be uttered by words ... It is the cause of being to all things, but itself is not, for it is beyond all being'. (*DN* c.1, 1) (Dionysius uses in the Greek the famous *epekeina* from the *Republic*.) As he explains in chapter five, 'God is not existent in any ordinary sense, but in a simple and undefinable manner embracing and anticipating all existence in himself'. (817D) Or again in chapter one: 'It is the cause of all beings and yet itself is nothing, hyperessentially transcending them all'. (593C)

But this insistence on the transcendence of God, on his unknowableness and ineffability, forces Dionysius to ask himself (*DN* c.1, 5) how then can there be any discussion of God. He answers that the praise of the Highest is best effected through the removal of all attributes. In chapter one of the *Mystical Theology* he advises Timothy to leave aside the senses and the operations of the intellect, and the objects of sense and intellect, and everything that is not and that is, and to strain as far as possible towards union, in a state of unknowing, with that which is above all being and knowledge, and so come to that ray of the Divine Darkness which is beyond all being. (933-999A) The journey toward the Divine Darkness is illustrated by a simile in chapter two: we do it by removing all the things that are, just as men who are carving out a statue remove all that stands in the way of the clear vision of the beauty that is still hidden, and so, through this removal and it alone, reveal the shape on its own, the hidden beauty. (1025 A-B) That is why the negative theology is preferred. For, as he says in the last chapter (c.13, 3) of the *Divine Names*, nothing associated with creatures can explain the hiddenness of that hyper-Godhead which transcends all. 'Even the name of "Goodness" we do not apply to it because we think it fitting, but only from the desire of forming some conception and saying something about its ineffable nature. And so we set aside for it in the first place the most honoured of names'. (981A) It is for this reason that men have preferred the ascent to it through negations.

'All human thought is a kind of error when set against the fixedness and stability of divine and perfect thoughts'. (*DN* 865B) The inadequacy of human language is felt more keenly in talk of God. But language does at least reveal the paradoxes which the existence of God poses for the human mind. (It need scarcely be emphasised that Dionysius has no hesitations about the fact of God's existence.) One of these paradoxes is the old one about the unmoved mover. Dionysius refers frequently to the unchangingness of God, but one has the impression that he is repeating a formula, sometimes in the paradoxical form (*et stans, et motus* in Eriugena's translation *DN* 1151B), which has never caused him any real difficulty. If he had read Marius Victorinus, he does not seem to have been disturbed by Candidus. (This applies also to his teaching on creation as we shall see.) He says (*DN* 916C) that talk of God going out to all things and moving is to be understood as meaning that God brings all things into being and continues them in being and exercises providence over them and is present to them – an explanation which, as Rolt says, is to be found in Augustine and which Eriugena himself takes up from Dionysius. He does not seem to be particularly concerned with an aspect of the unmoving problem which later bothered Eriugena, i.e. that if God is not moved, he is not moved by love. (*Periph.* 504B) Paradox is a stimulus to Dionysius more frequently than it is a difficulty.

Nevertheless there are difficulties in his system which Dionysius recognises explicitly. One of these is the problem of evil. This arises for him in a particularly awkward form because of his Neoplatonist emphasis on the world as an emanation from the One. The emanation position contrasts in turn with the Christian doctrine of creation from nothing, so it is better for us to begin there, at the beginning. We saw that in chapter five of the *Divine Names* Dionysius said that his purpose was not to reveal the Reality which is beyond Reality, because it was unknowable and unutterable. His purpose rather was to celebrate the emanation of the Divine essence (*tés thearchikés ousiarchias proodon*) into the universe of things. We saw also his language about the outpouring of light, and the continuation of the Platonic theme of the excess of goodness and the universe it produces. This might suggest that the overflow is an automatic process and so clashes with the notion of creation as a free act of God. But this does not seem to be a source of embarrassment for Dionysius. 'The truth we must proclaim above all others is that through his goodness, the Hyperessential Thearchy, having set down the essence of things, has brought them into existence'. (*CH* 177C) While insisting on the emanation, he still insists that God retains his unity and fullness, that he is not diminished by his outpouring. As he says in c. 2, 11 of the *Divine Names*: 'He is multiplied but in a manner which retains unity, he is made manifold from the one yet without going out from It. God is being hyper-essentially, and gives being to the things which are, and produces all reality, and that single One, which he is, is said to be made many by the production from himself of the many things that are, while he none the less remains One in the multiplication, and unified while the emanation goes on, and perfectly full in the separation out'. (*DN* 649B)

All things then proceed from God and are produced by him, in an ecstacy of love as it were, while he utterly transcends all things.

When we turn to examine more closely how this happens we meet again a familiar Platonist combination, the Forms and God. 'It must be granted that all the paradigms of existing things pre-exist in him, though in accordance with one hyper-essential unity; for it produces essences by an outgoing from essence. By 'paradigms' we mean those principles (*logoi*) which pre-exist in God and produce the essences of things in him as a unity. These principles theology calls 'predeterminings', divine and beneficial expressions of will, which define things and make them, and through these principles the Hyperessential Being pre-ordained and brought into existence all beings'. (DN c. 5,8, 824C and cf. 821A-B) 'In him is every paradigmatic principle, final, efficient, formal material all beginning, coherence and end'. (*DN* c.4, 10, 705D) (One can see here, by the way, that Dionysius' Platonism readily accepts Aristotelianism: the syncretism of these philosophies plus Stoicism which is to be found in Plotinus was continued down through the centuries in his successors.)

But if a good God has created the world, if it can be described as an overflow of his goodness, if everything that exists is built on a plan somehow found in him, how can there be evil? 'How can there be evils at all if Providence exists?' (*DN* c.4, 33, 7333) 'What is the origin of evil? In what does it exist? And how did he that exists will to produce it? And how, if willed, was he able to produce it? And if evil comes from some other cause, what other cause is there for things except the good? And how is there evil, when Providence exists? How does it come about at all, how is it not destroyed? And why does any of the existing things desire it instead of the Good?' (*DN* c.4, 18, 715A-B) Dionysius answers this old pre-Christian question in traditional and very Neoplatonic words. He begins by saying that if everything in the world comes from good, then nothing comes from evil. Evil in itself has no existence. But Good extends to things only insofar as they are capable of receiving it. 'The perfect Good extends even to the lowest things, and is entirely present to some, to others only to a lower pitch, and to others again only in the last degree, in accordance with the capacity of each'. (*DN* c.4, 20, 717D) Things possess some share of good whether they like it or not. To sum up, 'all things, insofar as they are, are both good and from the good, and insofar as they are deprived of the good are neither good nor do they have being'. (ibid. 720A-B) Dionysius proceeds to argue this point more concretely, using, for instance, the phenomenon of anger, or desire, the essence of which, he says, is order reduced to a minimum. The conclusion is that evil is non-existent: elsewhere the old Plotinian analogy of the light fading is used to dramatise the negative quality of evil. (c.4, 24)

This is the sort of argument we have met often before in Platonist thought, and the sort that is convincing on its own principles until confronted with the brute facts of existence. This may be the reason why Dionysius feels he has to continue to argue a point which he should consider sufficiently well established: There is no dualism: God is good and all things come from him, and since he is unchanging, good comes from him unchangingly. Nor can it be said that the various forms of being are evil. Even the demons are not by nature evil 'but only through a lack of angelic good'. (ibid. c.4 ,24, 725B) Similarly, human beings are not inherently evil, nor the animals, nor nature as a whole, nor our bodies, nor matter itself: for insofar as matter has existence at all it must come from the Good. And so, he says, evil in souls does not result from matter but from disorderly motion (another term which is apparently taken directly from Plato).

But where does the disorderly motion come from? Dionysius is eloquent on the negative qualities of evil but his answer to the question of the source of evil is no more satisfactory than any of those we have seen. Evil arises from weakness (ibid. c.4, 31, 733c), an answer we have already seen in Proclus. Human beings are free and Providence respects their nature. (ibid. c.4, 33, 733c) They are free also to be lazy and not to use the intelligence which they have been given. They do not wish to see the good which they should do, and do not exercise the knowledge which they have been given. (ibid. c.4, 35, 736A) Dionysius adds immediatly that he has written elsewhere on this matter, but it seems unlikely that this lost writing would have thrown any further light on the matter. One does not expect, of course, a solution to the problem, but from what we can see it appears that Dionysius followed well-established lines with regard to the question. He uses the traditional arguments to explain the existence of defects in the world, such as 'educational' or punitive or 'aesthetic'. 'Even when things turn out badly Providence makes good use of them, either for one's own benefit or that of others, for individual or common advantage, and it takes thought for each of the things which exist, individually'. (733B) It is in fact an indication of the Divine Goodness that it does not allow men to be distracted from higher things by excessive material comfort. (c.8, 8, 896B-C) He points out in DN c.4, 22 that one cannot talk of the angels, who are the representatives of God, as being in any real sense responsible for something bad happening: if they are called 'bad', it is only because they punish sinners. This recalls Plutarch's division of daemons in *Tranquility of Mind*. These angels are, therefore, to be thought of like magistrates who punish people for their misdemeanours. There is no point in having a guard dog which is gentle to every-body: the fierceness which is 'bad' for intruders is precisely the virtue for which its master values it. (ibid. c.4, 25)

Dionysius is not, of course, denying the existence of moral evil, and, that being so, he must as a Platonist, as well as a Christian, face the question whether virtue is rewarded and vice is punished. We have already seen that he declared that not even the demons are by nature evil. What then are we to make of the punishment stories, and particularly of eternal punishment for those who have done evil? We would know more clearly the mind of Dionysius on this question if we had the lost work on *Just and Divine Judgement* to which he refers at the end of chapter four of the *Divine Names*. The insistence on the goodness of existence and the attitude of his disciple, Eriugena, later, leads us to think that he would have taken an optimistic view of the capacity of all to return to the ultimate unity and harmony. 'There is nothing of all the things that are which has entirely fallen away from unity' he says in chapter 11, 5 of the *Divine Names*. The Perfect Peace gives the opportunity of being enjoyed to the very limits of the universe and links together all things. (ibid. c.11, 2, 952A) He quotes approvingly from *Hierotheus* and speaks of his mystical communion with the truth. (ibid. c.2, 9ff, 648B) Union with the Unknown, *theósis*, deification, is the aim of Dionysius' philosophising. In the *Celestial Hierarchy* (165A) he echoes Plato when he says that 'the aim of the hierarchy is the likening to, and union with, God, in so far as that is possible'. The divine power, he tells us (*DN* c.8, 5, 895A), 'bestows deification itself by giving a faculty for it to those who are deified'. We may agree with Rolt that 'Dionysius is unquestionably speaking of a psychological state to which he himself had been occasionally led'. (p 33)

This is the man whom Eriugena translated and who through this and later translations influenced so greatly medieval speculation about the divinity. But Eriugena was a very influential figure in his own right and to him we must now turn. We know somewhat more about his life than that of Dionysius, but again there are large portions about which we know nothing. He was an Irishman who came to the continent and there translated from Greek into Latin the works of Dionysius. Whether he learnt his Greek mainly in Ireland or the continent is an interesting and disputed question, but one which we do not have to consider here.[5] It appears that he came to the court of Charles the Bald in the 840s. He taught in the palace school and was much involved in the academic debates of his day, mainly theological. The first important work from him that we have is *On Predestination* from about 850. But of much more consequence for later generations was his translation of Dionysius which he started in about 860 and which gave an accurate account of his thought to a Europe which now and for the next few hundred years was largely Greekless. This work of translation strongly influenced his own major work, the *Periphyseon*, or *On the Division of Nature* which he wrote in the mid 860s. The *Periphyseon* was later condemned, and Pope Honorius III ordered that all copies of the book should be sent to Rome for burning in 1225. But until that time its influence was immense as Cappuyns has shown, and even after this date it did not simply disappear. (His translation of Dionysius was, of course, unaffected by the condemnation of *Periphyseon*). The *Periphyseon* was Eriugena's own composition but it was so strongly marked by his reading of Platonising Greek and Latin Christians (like Dionysius, Gregory of Nyssa, Maximus, Ambrose, Augustine and Boethius) that it can properly be considered as one of the main channels of Platonic influence to the Middle ages.

The work commences with the division of all things into those which are and those which are not, and a more elaborate four-fold division then follows.[6] As might be expected from such a keen student of Dionysius, Eriugena places great emphasis on the negative theology, which, they agree, is a better way of talking about God than the affirmative theology. He also follows a basically Neoplatonic scheme in his explanation of the relation between God and the world, which consists of a process of emergence from and return to the One (see 526A and Sheldon-William's note ad loc. on *Dialectic in Neoplatonism*). He talks of 'the gathering together into the One which begins from man and ascends through man to God himself, who is the beginning of all division and the end of all unification'. (531D-532A) He uses the Neoplatonic imagery of the fountain to explain emergence from and return to God in, for instance, 632 BC where he talks of the divine goodness flowing out first into the 'primordial causes', and from them into their products and thence returning into the fountain which is the source of everything, 'all that is and all that is not'. He touches on the same image in 952 B-C, where it is linked with the notion that goes back to the *Timaeus* of there being no jealousy in God, and there one could get the impression that it is inconceivable that God being good would refrain from the creation of other good things which must in the end return to him. The steps of this return are spelt out in 876A-B until we come finally to the stage where 'God will be all in all, when there will be nothing except God alone'.

But the nearness of God which is implied in this language must be set against the emphasis on the transcendence and remoteness of God which is a constant theme of the *Periphyseon*. The influence of Dionysius is again obvious and he quotes him again without specifying the source in 456A: 'There is no way of signifying by verb or noun or any other part of articulated speech how the supreme and causal essence of all things can be signified'. Eriugena uses Dionysius' 'hyper' language to indicate that it is impossible to desribe God, because of the misleading suggestions that are implied in ordinary language. So in 459D he says: 'God is called essence, but strictly speaking he is not essence: for to being is opposed not-being. Therefore he is *hyperousios*, that is, super essential. Again, he is called Goodness, but strictly speaking he is not goodness: for to goodness wickedness is opposed. Therefore he is *hypergathos*, that is more-than-God, and *hyperagathotés*, that is, more than goodness. He is called God, but he is not strictly speaking God: for to vision is opposed to blindness, and to him who sees he who does not see. Therefore he is *hypertheos*, that is, more-than-God – for *theos* is interpreted 'He who sees". Or again: 'The Divine is incomprehensible to all reason and all intellect, and therefore when we predicate heirs of him we do not say that he is; for being is from him but he is not himself being. For above this being after some manner there is More-than-Being, and absolute Being beyond language and understanding'. (482A-B) He calls not only on Dionysius for support (see 509), but also Maximus, whom he confuses with Gregory Nazianzen. (587A) In the latter passage we are urged to reverence in silence the God who is 'ineffable and above understanding and beyond all knowledge'. The word that is translated 'beyond' here is the *epekeina* of Plato's *Republic*, which is again applied to the Divine Wisdom in 669B-C. (We have, however, no reason to believe that Eriugena was aware that the ultimate source was the *Republic*, just as we have no reason to believe that he knew that Dionysius was drawing on the *Symposium* when Eriugena translated *DN* 701D-704A.)

It is not surprising, given Eriugena's consciousness of the inaccessibility of God, that he, like Dionysius, prefers the negative when he distinguishes 'the two branches of theology, the affirmative, which by the Greeks is called *kataphatiké*, and the negative, which is named *apophatiké*. The one, that is *apophatiké*, denies that the Divine Essence or Substance is any of the things that are, that is, of the things which can be discussed or understood; but the other, *kataphatiké*, predicates of it all the things that are, and for that reason is called affirmative – not that it affirms that it is any of the things that are, but because it teaches that all things which take their being from it can be predicated of it.' (458A-B) God is he 'Who is better known by not knowing'[7], of whom ignorance is the true knowledge, who is more truly and faithfully denied in all things than he is affirmed. For whatever negation you make about him will be a true negation, but not every affirmation you make will be a true affirmation: for if you show that he is this or that you will be proved wrong, for he is none of the existing things that can be spoken of or understood . But if you declare: 'He is not this nor that nor anything', you will be seen to speak the truth, for he is none of the things that are or of those that are not, and no one may draw near him who does not first, by perservering in the way of thought, abandon all the senses and the operations of the intellect, together with the sensibles and everything that is and that is not, and, having achieved a state of non-knowing, is not restored to the unity as far as is possible of Him who is above every essence and understanding, of whom there is neither reason nor understanding, who is neither name nor word'. (510BC) 'This is the prudent and catholic and salutary profession that is to be predicated of God: that first by the cataphatic, that is, by affirmation, we predicate all things of him, whether by nouns or by verbs, though not properly but in a metaphorical sense; then we deny by the apophatic, that is, by negation, that he is any of the things which by the cataphatic are predicated of him, only (this time) not metaphorically but properly – for there is more truth in saying that God is not any of the things that are predicated of him than in saying that he is; then, above everything that is predicated of him, his superessential nature which creates all things and is not created must be superessentially more than praised'. (522A-B) So negation is of more value than affirmation in investigating the sublimity and incomprehensibility of the Divine Nature. (684D, 758A) It is even true to say that God is truth and not truth, that he is whole and part and neither whole nor part. (757D, 759B)

The impossibility of saying anything properly about God does not prevent philosophers writing long books about him, as we've seen before in the case of Proclus particularly, and as the *Periphyseon* shows once again with nearly six hundred columns in Migne. God can only be expressed in paradoxes as the example of Augustine shows, particularly at the beginning of the *Confessions* (1, 4, 4) where he is, as so often, thinking Platonically not because of deliberate imitation but because Augustine is a Platonist by nature. Plato liked paradoxes because they forced people to think. Paradoxes are sometimes insoluble and all one can do is state them and leave them there. Some however are more fundamental and more challenging to ordinary experience and have to be faced. One of these is the paradox of the unmoving mover and it was obviously a paradox which perplexed Eriugena greatly. How can there be making or being made without some motion? If God is perfectly unmoving there is for the Christian a particularly acute problem because the scripture speaks of God making the world. Eriugena calls on Maximus for assistance. 'This venerable master,' he says, 'teaches that no motion is to be found except in those things which begin from an origin and proceed by their natural motion to their end'. (515C) We cannot speak of these two temini being separate in God for he can be referred to at once as the One Beginning-and-End of all things. (cf. 451D-452A) But there is a further consideration. 'Everything which lacks a beginning and an end necessarily lacks all motion also. But God is *anarchos*, that is, without beginning, because nothing precedes him or makes him to be; nor does he have an end because he is infinite: for it is understood that there is nothing after him since he is the limit of all things beyond which nothing proceeds. Therefore he does not admit any motion. For 'he has nowhere to move himself, since he is the fullness and the place and the perfection and the station and the Whole of all things, or rather, He is More-than-fullness-and-perfection, More-than-place-and-station, More-than-whole-of-all -things'. (516A-B)

This seems to establish that God is unmoving. Yet he is the maker of all things, and how can one have making without motion? There are no accidents in God: he is not a composite, but simple and perfect. 'So when we hear that God makes all things we ought to understand nothing else than that God is in all things, that is, that he is the essence of all things'. This is essentially the solution of Dionysius whom he quotes before he concludes this long and repetitive section. The conclusion reads: 'Just as being is predicated of him although he is not in the strict sense being because he is more than being and is the cause of all being and essence and substance, so also he is said to act and to make although he is more

than acting and making and is the cause of all for making and acting without any motion that could be attributed to accident, being
beyond all motion ... It is altogether necessary that, just as strictly
speaking being as well as acting and making are removed from
him, so suffering and being made are removed. For how that
which is not liable to acting and making can be liable to suffering
and being made I do not see'. (524A-B) 'Set an end to the book: for
there is enough contained in it', the alumnus hastens to request.

The very length of the treatment indicates Eriugena's unease at
the problem which confronts him, and nowhere is the unease
more obvious than in his discussion in this section of one very important form of motion, love. It is the first question he raises when
earlier in Book One he commences his examination of the Aristotelian categories of acting and being acted upon. If God, as
agreed, neither moves nor is moved, he neither loves nor is loved.
This to Eriugena is a very strange conclusion indeed and against it
is ranged the authority of all the Holy Scriptures and the holy
Fathers. 'But if God loves what he makes he is surely seen to be
moved; for he is moved by his love. And if he is loved by those
who can love whether they know what they love or do not know
it, is it not certain that he moves them?' (505A) Some long digres-
sions on different topics ensue before he returns to the problem of
God's love in 512D: 'If God is called Love by metaphor although
he is more-than-love and surpasses all love, why should he not in
the same way be said to love although he surpasses every motion
of loving?' But Eriugena is aware that this is a general remark on
the inadequacy of language rather than an answer to the specific
question he is faced with and he continues his discussion. He
takes as definition of love 'a bond and chain by which the totality
of all things is bound together in ineffable friendship and indissoluble unity' or 'the end and quiet resting place of the natural motion of all things that are in motion, beyond which no motion of
the creature extends'. (519B) These descriptions of love are supported from Dionysius' *Hierotheos*, and Eriugena concludes:
'Rightly therefore is God called Love since he is the cause of all
love and is diffused thro' all things and gathers all things together
into one and involves them in himself in an ineffable return, and
brings to an end in himself the motions of love of the whole creature'. (519D-520A)

But he still has to answer the question of how God loves or is
loved. He now says that God is said to be loved by that he has
made, not because anything is done to him by them, 'but because
all things seek him and because his beauty draws all things to

himself'. (5203) He is not moved any more than is he magnet which attracts iron. Or again God is like the light which so fills the world that it is unmoving, yet seems to be moved because it causes animals to see, or like a body of knowledge which is unchanging yet has the power to move those who acquire it. We are, therefore, left again with similes which, though attractive in themselves, create, as often, the impression that a problem is being explained away rather than explained.

The question of God's moving is, of course, closely connected as we said with the process of creation and Eriugena combines what appears to be the Christian expression of the concept of creation from nothing with a Platonist version of the further developments. In 952B he talks of how 'all things were made from nothing' through the Supreme Good, the *Summum Bonum*. This Supreme Good 'created existing things from non-existing'. But, as remarked earlier, one could get the impression from this very passage that it is a Platonist who is speaking in the tradition of the *Timaeus*, that it is irconceivable that God being good could refrain from the creation of other good things. And on further investigation one discovers that Eriugena's notion of 'creation from nothing' is different from what might be taken to be a normal understanding of this view. For in spite of his emphasis that before things were made they did not exist (636A), and that through generation they began to exist in time as what they were not before, he also says that things created in their primordial causes were there eternally. (665A-B) As might be expected from Eriugena, he faces himself with the dilemma put in the mouth of the alumnus: 'If all the things which exist are eternal in the creative wisdom, how are they made from nothing?' (636A)

It emerges that 'nothing' has the meaning that Eriugena has derived from Dionysius' negative theology. The primordial causes, which are also called the Ideas or Forms, are in God and are the 'formulae', so to speak, of existing things which in this way come from God. But God, as we saw, is described better by the negative than by the affirmlative theology: He is so far beyond being that he is better described as 'Nothing'. (581C-684D) So God by making things from himself creates them from nothing, although of course the Divine Superessentiality as 'nothing' means 'more than being'. (634R)

He creates through the 'primordial courses'. A summary description of these, dependent again on Dionysius, is given at 615D: 'The primordial causes are what the Greeks call *ideai*, that is, the eternal species or forms and immutable reasons after which and in which the visible and invisible world is formed and governed; and therefore they were appropriately named by the wise men of the Greeks *prototypa*, that is, the principal exemplars which the Father made ... They are also called *proorismata*, that is, predestinations. For in them whatever is being and has been and shall be made by divine providence is at one and the same time and immutably predestined ... They are also customarily called by the philosophers *theia thelemata*, that is, divine volitions, because everything that God wished to make he made in them primordially and causally; ... all things subsist by participation in them, while they themselves are participations of the one cause of all things ... and they are said to be through themselves for the reason that no creature is interposed between them and the one cause of all things; and while they subsist immutably in it they are the primordial causes of other causes that come after them, to the uttermost bounds of the whole of nature, even multiplied to infinity'. He then gives as examples of the primordial causes goodness-through-itself, being, life, wisdom, truth, intellect, reason, power, justice, health, omnipotence, eternity, peace (each through itself), which sound like an enlarged list of Plato's *megista gené*, the greatest classes, under which all other *genera* and species must fall, but which are backed, in fact, he says, by the authority of Dionysius in the *Divine Names*.

We saw earlier that in 532 B-C Eriugena uses the Neoplatonic imagery of the fountain to describe the divine goodness flowing out first into the 'primordial causes', and from them into their products, from whence there is the return. All good, essence, life, sense, reason, wisdom, genus, species, beauty, order, unity, equality, difference, place, time (a list similar to the one we have just seen), have their source in this fountain which is the Suprere Goodness. It is the cause of all things, is all things. For, as he says, 'if the intelligising (*intellectus*) of all things is all things, Goodness alone has all things in its intellect (*ipsa sola intelligit omnia*); therefore it alone is all things'. (632D) It alone truly is; the other things, which are said to be, are theophanies (or manifestations) of it'. And Eriugena uses not only this Neoplatonist progression from the Good to Mind, but the favourite illustrations for God and world relations of One and numbers, centre and circle, point and line, light and its diffusion. (621C,705C)

Once again, the perfection of this planning and progression raises the question of the source of the imperfection, the problem of evil in a world that derives from the good. Eriugena says (808C) that the irrational mutability of free will is the cause of evil. But free will has been given to man who, as he said earlier in *De Praed*, 373B, has been made in the image of God and therefore must be free to allow him to show his virtue by choosing the good. Man, however, makes mistakes, and through his own perverseness misuses the good to his own disadvantage. (828D) Considered in itself, evil is absolutely nothing except an irrational and perverse and imperfect movement of a rational nature: It is shifting and causeless and has no real existence. Eriugena's discussions of the question are obviously Neoplatonic with one of the main channels being in this case Augustine (see esp. *De Praed*. 395Cff). His work *De Libero Arbitrio* is quoted when Eriugena deals with a connected difficulty in this area, which is that, if God knows all things, including future events, and if he cannot be wrong, does not his foreknowledge predetermine what is to happen and therefore render any talk of man's free-will meaningless? In the passage which Eriugena quotes approvingly (*De Praed*. 375Cff) Augustine uses the parallel of memory and prescience: just, he says, as you do not force things to have taken place because you remember them, so too God does not force things to happen simply because he knows they will happen in the future. And just as you remember some things which you did and nevertheless did not do all the things which you remember, so too God has foreknowledge of all the things of which he is the author but is not himself the author of all things of which he has foreknowledge.

The easy but unconvincing optimism of this explanation of man's moral evil is continued in the explanation of evil in the universe. Here again Eriugena is glad to fall back on Augustine and the 'aesthetic' argument for the existence of evil. This he refers to briefly in Book One of the *Periphyseon*: 'God gathers and puts all these things together by a beautiful and ineffable harmony into a single concord: for those things which in the parts of the universe seem to be opposed and contrary to one another and to be discordant with one another are in accord and in tune when they are viewed in the most general harmony of the universe itself'. (517C) He elaborates the argument in the final book of that work, Book Five, where he quotes Augustine on the effectiveness of a dark colour among brighter colours in a picture. (953Cff) One must take an overall view and when one does that which might seem ugly when considered partially and by itself is found to enhance the whole picture.

Evil does not, indeed, seem important in the universe of Eriugena where the triumph of good is assured. 'All the things that exist exist to the extent that they are good'. (628A) He there argues that eternal existence implies goodness. That raises the question of the eternity of punishment for evil and the nature of the punishment. That raises a question requiring much caution and Eriugena is duly cautious. On this occasion he calls on another great authority, Ambrose, to back his view that the punishment will be not corporal or local or sensible or temporal but psychological. Judas is tortured in his own polluted conscience and his punishment is that of a late and useless repentence which burns always within him. Herod too is consumed with the flame of his own mad fury which raged against the innocents. (936Aff) The torturing will be due to memory and conscience. (964D) 'The name of all these torments (fire, worms)', as he says later (971A), 'are used figuratively in sacred scripture, as Saint Ambrose testifies,' and as the Greek words which are used on the occasion indicate.

Yet the return of all things to the One which Eriugena emphasises frequently (see also 683Bff) seems to demand more than the removal of physical punishment. Eriugena talks of every creature being saved and being restored to the ineffable unity. (913) And he quotes another great authority, 'the theologian Gregory' (of Nyssa), to support his contention that 'evil (*malitia*) cannot be perpetual, but in the neccessity of things it will come to a fixed terminus and will at some time cease. For if the divine goodness ... is eternal and infinite, its contrary will of necessity not be eternal and infinite ... Evil will be entirely abolished, and the irrational movements of the human spirit will be changed into rational love of the truth'. (918) This prompts the editor of the Migne text, Floss, to write one of his rare footnotes: 'We need hardly remind you that what Joannes Scotus says about the abolition of evil and about the punishments and sufferings of the impious, whether human beings or demons etc., is completely at variance with Catholic truth'.

The world will be dissolved and will return into its causes. (925B) 'Nature with its causes will pass into God, as air passes into light'. (867A-B) The body will pass into the soul which is its cause and the rational soul which is the image of God will turn into God himself, the one cause of all things. The reward for merit briefly, he says, will be *theosis*, that is, deification. (972C-3) We shall all be restored to unity and the unity will exist in spite of the differences of merit and defects, just as in one single big house there are all classes and conditions of men included. Using biblical language he says that we will all be restored to 'paradise', that is, to the pristine dignity of our condition, but only those who are worthy of deification will participate of the tree of life. All will have their dwellings, whether they have lived well or ill in the flesh. (982C) There will be the ineffable ascent to God himself and God will be all in all. (lC21)

Eriugena is long-winded and repetitive, and the *Periphyseon* is not particularly attractive reading in either Latin or English. But he does seem honest and acute, and Sheldon-William's estimate of his importance seems justified and is shared by other scholars. The size of the *Periphyseon* together with his translations made him a most important channel in the period for the transition of Greek thought to the medieval Western world. The only authorities to whom he gives credit by name are Christians, but we cannot rule out others,[8] especially when we take Dionysius into account. The very nature of the pious fraud which Dionysius is perpetrating confines his explicit references to the very highest Christian company of the first Christian century, but later scholarship has naturally broadened the list of borrowings. We saw that the confusion lasted, by and large, until the fifteenth century. But one has the feeling that even before then intelligent men had their suspicions, even if piety restrained them from voicing them openly. Thomas Aquinas wrote a commentary on Dionysius' *Divine Names*, and in the prologue to that he explains that there are difficulties in Dionysius' books for many reasons. The first of these is that 'generally he uses a style and manner of speaking which the Platonists used, which is unusual for moderns'. He gives us what he regards as clear examples of the Platonic style of speaking in the first part of his commentary on chapter five and says that it is because of this (*propter hoc*) that Dionysius uses certain language about being and mind.[9] The Latin term for the Platonists, *Platonici*, which Aquinas uses, could be applied to Plato and his immediate school as well as the Neoplatonists, but it does seem as if St Thomas might have suspected that Dionysius was writing much later than he pretended.

That he was doing so has been shown decisively since, particulally through the efforts of Koch and Stigimayr, who made it quite clear, in 1895, that Dionysius at the end of chapter four of the *Divine Names* was following closely *De malorum subsistentia* of Proclus.[10] The evidence of dependence on the Neoplatonists and particularly on Iamblichus and Proclus could be and soon was extended. Dionysius' development of triads drew on them, and Koch has shown that he often used even identical formulae. But while all this may be obvious to nineteenth and twentieth century readers of Greek who have the texts in front of them, it escaped the notice of the contemporaries of Eriugena and their successors for centuries afterwards. The importance of Dionysius to the Western world, originally through the translations of Eriugena, is something we now find hard to credit, but that is only a further reason for re-stating it. There were further translations and commentaries, and even when Eriugena's *Periphyseon* was condemned, the work of Dionysius continued to mark the Scholastic systems.

The *Periphyseon* was not condemned until the beginning of the thirteenth century, and by the year 1225, the year in which Pope Honorius III ordered all copies to be sent to Rome for burning, St Thomas Aquinas had been born. The *Periphyseon* had had a vigorous life for over three hundred years. According to Pope Honorius its use was still very widespread in monasteries and places of study at the beginning of the thirteenth century. The golden age of its influence was probably over anyway, even if the burning had not been ordered, because of the growing popularity of the new method of the *Summae* and of the dialectical style of the technical works of Aristotle and the 'new logic' which underlay the *Summae*. But the order for burning did not mean that the *Periphyseon* simply disappeared. Copies were preserved, as we know, and the work on a modern critical edition still goes on. Even without the full text the name of Eriugena could not simply be wiped out. He remained an authority, even if under a shadow, and we may conclude, as we started, with Sheldon-Williams, that Eriugena has been 'a formative influence in the tradition not only of Western mysticism, but also of medieval scholasticism'.

CHAPTER 9

St Thomas Aquinas and the Greek Tradition

Eriugena is the last thinker we wish to consider in this history of the transmission of Greek philosophical thought to Christian natural theology. Eriugena was in any case the outstanding thinker in half a millenium, but what is of interest to us is that he was the last example of the combination in one person of important thinker and translator-transmitter of the Greek inheritance. Two centuries elapsed before Anselm appeared. But great as Anselem was, and Abelard after him, they had no direct access to the Greek tradition. So, however great their achievements in other directions, they must fall outside our scope. Similarly, however great was the devotion of the school of Chartres to what they knew of Plato, their contribution to the mainstream of Western natural theology was not sufficiently important to warrant our attention in a book of this size.

The representative figure in the history of medieval thought after Eriugena is Thomas Aquinas. Even to near contemporaries it seemed that he and Bonaventure were the two leading thinkers of their age. The centuries since then have confirmed his superiority through the amount of both adulation and vituperation which he has received. His position of eminence was due in the first place to his own genius, belied as it was by his appearance (he was sometimes called 'the dumb ox') and not exhibited in the flashier types of controversy much favoured in his day. But Thomas was also fortunate in the time at which he was born. Scholasticism to us suggests dead pedantry, the counting of angels on heads of pins etc., but in 1200 AD it was the still fresh and developing style of thinking, stimulated by the flow of translations of the 'new' writings of Aristotle. St Thomas' time is described as the age of the rediscovery of Aristotle. Aristotle and Aquinas were linked together in the centuries to come, and the rejection of 'Scholasticism' in the various enlightenments often meant the rejection of Aristotle. Aquinas refers to him most frequently as, simply, *philosophus*, the Philosopher, as if he exhausted his species, or as one might refer to *The Man Above*. This has given rise to some misunderstanding which it is the purpose of this chapter to dispel.

The twelfth century, the century before that of Aquinas, saw the first great steps in the work of translating the bulk of the writings of Aristotle, other than the small body of the old logic which as we have seen had always survived.[1] The main channel of this work was Spain, where a high civilisation, both Arabic and Jewish, had, through its international connections, preserved and handed on the thought of the great Greek philosophers. Gerard of Cremona (1114-1187) was the most influential of these translators in the twelfth century, and from that time on the flood of Aristotelianism was unstoppable.

Thomas Aquinas was born in 1224-5, and studied at Monte Cassino, Naples, Paris and Cologne. Albert the Great, a most learned man, was his master (he was born in 1206), and Albert, while far from being simply an Aristotelian, was well aware of the advancing Aristotelianism of his day. Albert insisted that Christians should make use of the best philosophical and scientific learning of the time, and we have his own statement of his intention to rewrite Aristotle, adding to him and improving him where necessary.[2] Augustine, Boethius and Dionysius were among the authors he used for the latter purpose. He must have made a deep impression on Thomas while he studied under Albert in Paris from 1245-1248 and in Cologne from 1248-1252. At a later stage, while Thomas was with Pope Urban IV at Orvieto in 1261-1264, he was to meet the greatest translator of the thirteenth century, William of Moerbeke, during the time while, it is reckoned, he was writing the *Summa Contra Gentiles* and before the writing of the *Summa Theologiae*.

We can expect, then, to meet Aristotelianism in the works of St Thomas and we are not disappointed. It is, of course, Aristotle as understood by another great genius, but Aquinas had studied his translations of Aristotle closely. That is apparent from the many commentaries we have from him on the works of Aristotle. But more important in the history of thought and of more interest to us are the great works, particularly the two *Summae*, where he gives his own views on what we have been calling natural theology (whether Thomas himself would agree with this title is another question which we do not need to discuss here). It has often been taken that Aquinas here sets out straight Aristotelianism, and while it is understandable that this view should be taken, it does, nevertheless, require some correction.

It is understandable that the view should be taken because when Aquinas sets out to give the reasons to prove that God exists in the *Summa contra Gentiles* I, 13, he begins by saying: 'Let us give first the reasons by which Aristotle proceeds to prove that God exists. He endeavours to prove this from the consideration of movement, in two ways'. He first argues back to the unmoved mover, 'and this we call God', Aquinas says. He cites the *Physics* frequently in establishing this first point, and he also devotes a paragraph to showing that there is no real discrepancy between Plato and Aristotle concerning a first mover. The second way taken from Aristotle depends on a consideration of necessity and contingence, and here again the *Physics* and the metaphysics are cited.

By far the most famous proofs, however, of the existence of God in Aquinas are those given in the *Summa Theologiae*, the Five Ways, in Ia, 2, 3. The five ways are from movement, the efficient cause, the possible and the necessary (or from contingency), degrees, and the government of things. In the explanation of the first way, based on the analysis of movements, Aristotle is not explicitly mentioned, but the parallel passage from *SCG* which we have glanced at establishes beyond reasonable doubt that Aristotle is the source of Aquinas' argument. The second way, from the notion of efficient cause, depends on a distinction of ways of explaining things (their 'causes') first made explicit by Aristotle, and is obviously closely connected with the first way: it is necessary to suppose some first efficient cause, and this everyone calls 'God'. The third way says that we know from experience that some things have the possibility of being or not being. But if everything has the possibility of not being, at some time there was nothing. So we have to presume that there is something which is necessary of itself and does not have the cause of its necessity outside itself, but is the cause of necessity for other things, and this we call God. This way again appears to be based primarily on Aristotle and his commentators.

The fourth way is the only one which cites Aristotle specifically, with a reference to the *Metaphysics*. And yet, even though, as Kenny says, 'admirers of Aquinas are divided in their attitude to the fourth way', 'all agree, however, that it is the way in which, for better or worse, St Thomas comes closest to Platonism.'[3] It is the argument from degrees in things. A thing may be more or less good than others, or true, or noble and so on. But things are said to be 'more' or 'less', depending on their distance from a maximum, such as 'most hot'. There is therefore something which is truest and best and noblest, and consequently 'most being', *maxime ens*, for, as is said in the second book of the *Metaphysics*, what is most true is most being. But the maximum in such a case is the cause of everything else there, as for example in the case of fire and hot. Therefore there is something which is the cause of being and goodness and any perfection whatsoever in things, and this we call God. We saw that there occurs among the fragments attributed to Aristotle the following argument: 'Where there is a better, there is a best; among existing things one is better than another; therefore there is a best, which must be the divine'.[4] It may, therefore, at first seem surprising that the admirers of Aquinas to whom Kenny refers agree that in the fourth way Aquinas comes closest to Platonism. But in the first place Aristotle is often himself (implicitly) relying on a Platonic form of argumentation, and in the second, as Kenny well shows, Aquinas is drawing on the Platonic notion of being and the Platonic theory of Forms to support the reasoning he here presents. That the results were not philosophically happy is another question; what we wish to emphasise here is that the fourth way is another indication that the return of Aristotelianism in the twelfth and thirteenth centuries by no means implied the removal of the Platonism that had been dominant in theological speculation up to then.

The fifth way is taken from the governance of things. Natural bodies act for an end. But things do not act for an end without some direction of awareness or intelligence. There is therefore something intelligent by which all natural things are ordered to an end, and this we call God. No authority is cited to support this, but it recalls immediately one of the oldest and most popular arguments for the existence of a good God or gods, the argument from design or teleology. Aquinas' exposition recalls elements from the Platonic and Stoic arguments for providence as well as the insistence in Aristotle that God and nature do nothing without a purpose. This popular argument had also, as we have seen, provoked much opposition, stretching back to Empedocles and including Theophrastus as well as the Epicureans. Aquinas, however, takes no account of such opposition here. His statement of the argument is almost as bald as that here given. Indeed, the five ways all together take up so little space in the voluminous writings of Aquinas that the question has been asked what his intention was in putting them forward and whether he seriously intended them as 'proofs' for the existence of God.

That again is, luckily, a question that does not concern us. We have listed them merely to show that they do not represent as big a break with the till then predominantly Platonic tradition as was sometimes supposed. Aquinas uses Aristotelian language but the underlying thought is in any case as much Platonist as Aristotelian. We have seen that in the fourth and fifth ways. The first three ways also owe a great deal to Plato's discussions of the primacy of soul over body and particular the primacy and necessity of the soul as the initiator of every sort of movement.

That same tendency to mingle Platonism and Aristotelianism is to be found elsewhere in his 'natural' theology. Aquinas' admiration for Aristotle and his following of Aristotle in criticism of specific points in Plato's system, including one aspect of the Theory of Forms, did not prevent him from making distinctions in favour of Plato. 'The opinion of the Platonists is most true and in accordance with the Christian faith in regard to what they said about the first principle of things', he says in the prologue to the *Divine Names* which we have already referred to. It should, however, be stated that 'the Platonists' is a rather vague term with Aquinas, and we can seldom claim that he is giving credit to Plato himself, rather than his followers. Nor may we be dogmatic in claiming that Aquinas recognised in a Christian author what we see as a piece of the Platonic or Neoplatonic inheritance; sometimes simply we do not know, and we should remain aware of that.

That he would praise the Platonists for calling God goodness, unity and truth hardly needs mentioning: more interesting, as we shall see, is his combination of justifications for the Greek ways of talking about God. But before turning to that we may take a brief glance at Aquinas' use of the tradition. That God is good, is one and is the truth is argued in chapters 37, 42 and 60 respectively of Book One of the *Summa Contra Gentiles*. That God is good is argued from the *Physics*, *Ethics* and *Metaphysics* of Aristotle, because God is perfect, the first unmoved mover as first object of desire, and the object of all desire as the always actual reality. And even when Aquinas talks about the communication of good he explains it in Aristotelian terms, and quotes *bonum diffusivum sui* without the slightest nod to Platonism. And in chapter 42, that God is one, among more Aristotelian argumentation there occurs what is perhaps another eloquent silence: the corporeal is ordered to the spiritual, which will be ultimately one and this is what we mean by God, he says. He does not add that this line of thought might be found in Eriugena. Similarly, Platonist argumentation is used to show that God is truth (c. 60), but the only authorities quoted are 'the Philosopher' and Avicenna.

The *Summa Contra Gentiles* also offers us interesting examples of how Aquinas combines Greek theories on speaking about God. In chapter thirty of Book One he begins to discuss the names that can be predicated of God. In the first place, names which indicate perfection absolutely and without any defect can be used of God, as they can be used elsewhere. These are names like goodness, wisdom, being, etc. which are used of creatures, but used of God in a supereminent fashion. Other names may be used only metaphorically of God, just as we use names of things metaphorically of human beings – a rough diamond is an example we might use. Finally, some names express perfections in such a supereminent way that they can be used of God alone: these are names like 'the Highest Good', 'the First Being' and so on.

The three ways of analogy, negation and eminence are, as we have seen, part of Platonism from the very beginning, derived from the central portion of the *Republic*, and available in handbook form at least by the time of Albinus as justifications for talking about God. Aquinas refers to the way of negation at the end of this chapter where he explains that names can signify perfections about God in the way of supereminence only through negation, as when we say that God is eternal or infinite, or through relation to other things, when he is said to be the first gauge or the highest good. But his primary source for such distinction was not, of course, the *Republic*, or Albinus, but Dionysius in whon he is steeped. He wrote a commentary on the *Divine Names*, but even more striking is his constant reference to Dionysius in, for instance, the *Summa Theologiae* where one gains the impression that 'the Philosopher', Augustine and Dionysius are, after the bible, his favourite reading. He tells us in the commentary or the *Divine Names* how negation, eminence and analogy are divided in the works of Dionysius: the first (*per remotionem*) is dealt with in the *Mystical Theology*; the second, through the intelligible processions' in this book, i.e. the *Divine Names*; and the third, 'through sense likenesses' in the book on *Symbolic Theology*. We saw that he indicates the proofs for God's existence in chapter 13 of *SCG*, I: in the following chapter, 14, he shows his approval of Dionysius' preference for the way of negation as he argues that, given that there is a God, we should best use the way of negation in coming to know Him. 'We cannot grasp the divine substance by knowing what it is, but we have some knowledge of it by learning what it is not'. Similarly, in the *Summa Theologiae*: la, 2, 3 gives us the five ways to prove the existence of God, but that established, the introduction to Question 3 which follows immediately says: 'But since we cannot know about God what he is, but what he is not, we cannot now reflect about God, how he is, but rather how he is not'.

Aquinas shows his sympathy with the negative way tradition in a further distinction which he makes (*SCG* 1, 30; *ST* la, 13, 3).

This is between the perfection signified of God and the mode of signification. For some names may signify perfection without defect as we saw, but the manner of signifying this will always be defective. This is because of the limitations of our understanding and our language. So, he says, as Dionysius teaches, names of this sort can be both affirmed and denied of God: affirmed because of the content, and denied because of the manner.

But the preference for the negative way in the Neoplatonist tradition is balanced in Aquinas by the influence of 'the Philosopher', though once again Thomas does not think of balancing but rather of broadening and filling out our ways of talking about God. This influence could be described as simply another form of the Platonist way of analogy, and Thomas used the term, but that would not be giving Aristotle his due. Aquinas says that terms are used of God and creatures neither univocally nor purely equivocally but by analogy or proportion. (*SCG* 1, 32ff; *ST* la, l3, 5) His inspiration for this is evidently Book Gamma of the *Metaphysics* where Aristotle explains (1003a 33ff) that 'Being' is used in various senses, but all that 'is' is related to one central point, one definite kind of thing, just as everything that is 'healthy' is related to health. Aquinas uses the same illustration concretely and elaborates it.

The increased importance of analogical predication means that there is in Thomas less of the Neoplatonic insistence on the transcendence and ineffability of God and more on the diffusion of his goodness. But even though Aquinas uses the Platonic *bonum diffusivum sui* motif, he does not seem to be conscious of it as Platonic. It had been used so frequently by Christians through the Platonising centuries that it was accepted as simply Christian. Aquinas therefore can write the following in his commentary on the *Divine Names* (c.1, 1.2, p 266 col.l Parma): 'We know two things through the divine names which are handed on to us in the sacred scriptures, firstly the diffusion of the holy light and of any kind of goodness or perfection, and secondly the very principle of this diffusion; as for instance when we speak of the living God, we know of the diffusion of life in creatures and that the principle of this diffusion is God'. The second book of the *Summa Contra Gentiles* considers God's creation and his creatures, and while Aquinas insists on God's freedom in creation, he also talks a great deal about the diffusion of his goodness. He tells us that the divine goodness was the prime motive for creation 'according to Augustine who says: "We exist because God is good"'. (2, 28) Augustine is quoted twice to the same effect but with a slight variation in the wording in the *Summa Theologiae* 1a, 5, 1 and 13, 2; and in 1a, 5, 4 *bonum est diffusivum sui esse* is accepted as an axiom from the words of Dionysius. The principle of the *Timaeus* has become part of Christianity.

Platonism is also invoked in an explanation of the relation between God and his creation. We have seen that Thomas following Aristotle was critical of Plato's Theory of Forms from the epistemological and ontological point of view (see, e.g., *SCG* 3 24 and *ST* 1a ,6, 4). But on the other hand, as Kenny has well shown, 'he sometimes seems to make an implicit appeal to the theory;' and at other times he explicitly calls on it, to use it for his own purposes. He discusses how the one Divine Mind knows the many parts of his creation, for instance, and quotes Augustine who says that God made man in one way and horse in another, and that the schemes of things, the *rationes rerum* exist manifold in the Divine Mind. 'And so', he ends, 'there is some justification for the opinion of Plato which states that there are ideas, in accordance with which all the things that exist in the material world are formed'. (*SCG* 1, 54) He had started this discussion of God's knowledge of other things a few chapters earlier and had quoted Dionysius' *Divine Names* to support his view that God knows himself and 'other things as it were seen in his essence'. (*SCG* 1, 49) The forms of things must be in the divine intellect, he says. (ibid. 51) He also discusses God's knowledge in the *Summa Theologiae* and in the introduction to the *quaestio* on this topic explains that 'since all known is in the knower, and the schemes of things, the *rationes rerum*, inasmuch as they are in God knowing, are called *ideae*, some consideration of the ideas will have to be added to the consideration of knowledge'. (1a, 14) In the actual consideration of ideas, he quotes from Augustine's *83 Questions* as his authority for the existence of ideas and adds immediately in answer to three objections 'I reply that it must be said that it is necessary to posit ideas in the Divine Mind'. He argues that ideas must exist as examplars and as principles of knowledge. But he approves of Aristotle's criticism of Plato for positing the independent existance of ideas, rather than their existence in the mind. (1a, 14, 1)

That this account might give a misleading impression of the positions of both Plato and Aristotle is obvious. But Aquinas, it must be repeated, is not concerned with giving a history of thought nor with meticulous *Quellenforschung*. He is again arguing a point which had become part of the Christian tradition. Plato is used or misused for this purpose, and insofar as he is given credit, it is for seeing something which Aquinas takes to be an obvious truth. The nature of his approach is best seen by his use of authorities in this *quaestio*. Augustine's *83 Questions* is regarded as an irreproachable source: there is no suggestion that the value of this work might be lessened through being at best third-hand.

Finally, we shall glance at a question which has been discussed by the pagans down through the centuries since Plato and had been particularly agonising for Aquinas' great Christian master, Augustine, the problem of evil. Aquinas as we might expect is convinced of God's providence, and drew on Platonist material to support his belief. In his commentary on the *Divine Names* he outlines five views of providence, those of the Epicureans, certain Peripatetics, the Stoics, some Egyptians, and some Platonists. He says that we may accept only the fifth, that of some Platonists, if we are to make sense of prayer. This view is that divine providence is unchanging but that some things in a changing and contingent state are contained within it. (c3, 1.1, p 292 cl Parma) This is the view followed by Dionysius, but the nature of his commentary does not allow Aquinas to give the matter systematic treatment here. This is to be found in the two *Summae*. (SCG 3, 64ff; ST 1a ,22) In SCG 3, 71 he wants to show 'that divine providence does not totally exclude evil from things'.

This chapter contains seven arguments to explain the existence of evil under a good God, but it presumes an awareness of other discussions. It does not, then, need to follow the logical order, so a little switching round of the order of the arguments makes it easier for us to read. Created things must be allowed to act according to their proper nature. So God allows his creatures to work with him in the universe. The performance of even the perfect artist can be spoiled by a defect in his instrument. And that is how it happens with God. Yet we can see providence in this also. For in the created world variety is necessary for perfect goodness: there must be an order in goodness. (cf SCG 2, 39) If this order did not exist, it would take from the fullness of things and the perfection of the creature. So there must be a possibility of declining from goodness and on this evil follows. Besides, even when evil is done, good is intended. If providence ruled out the intention of some good in a universal manner, much good would be taken out of the universe. So fire should not be stopped burning even though there follows the destruction of what is burned. (cf ST 1a, 22, 2) Moreover, evils give room for the play of good, which would not exist without them. If we did not have the viciousness of persecutors we would not have the virtue of the long-suffering of the last. (cf ST 1a, 22, 2; 48, 2) A further point is that we must think of the overall picture, the beauty of which comes from the harmony, through contrast, of good and evil. Finally, evil helps us appreciate good which we might otherwise neglect, just as we never think of good health until we are sick. (cf ST 1a, 2, 3 ad.l)

There is not much novelty in all this. Many of the arguments go back at least as far as the Stoics, who in turn were drawing on Plato and Aristotle. The parallels (I do not claim more than that) to Plotinus' treatise on providence (*Enneads* III 2) are striking. Nor is there much more novelty in his answer in the *Summa Theologiae* to the old objection to providence, that 'many just people are afflicted in this world'. For the answer is that through afflictions of this kind some small faults are purified in them, and they are more stimulated towards God and away from liking for earthly things, (1a, 21, 4) The material is traditional and a glance at the authorities he adds as a form of footnote (*SCG* 3, 83) will also show how Platonist it is – Gregory, Boethius, Dionysius and Augustine are all mentioned. To call the material traditional is not a reflection on Aquinas' originality but rather an indication of the intractability of the problem. The debates about predestination which had been raging for centuries had contributed heat (sometimes literally) rather than light. When Aquinas is discussing the question of God's knowledge of future contingents he is still using Boethius' image though he does not here mention his name. We know things in time sequence: God's knowledge is eternal. 'We are 'just like the man who walks along the road, he does not see those who come after him; but one who from a height looks down on the whole road, sees all together all who are travelling on it'. (*ST* 1a, 14, 13 ad 3)

We find, then, in Aquinas the continuation of the process of fusion of thought which had been going on for centuries in Greek and which now came together in one great system into Latin. It has been said that Neoplatonism could as well be called Neoaristotelianism. That is the sort of exaggeration that provokes thought. A similar sort of exaggeration, but in reverse, should make us remember the amount of Platonism which is present in so strong an Aristotelian as Aquinas. This was only to be expected. I have already remarked how it strikes one that, apart from the Scriptures, Dionysius and Augustine are the most frequently cited authorities with Aristotle. Aquinas knew that Dionysius was using Platonic language even if he does not call him a Platonist. We in this century particularly are aware how much a Platonist was Augustine. St Thomas was certainly not aware to the same extent and frequently drank in Platonism unsuspectingly. Boethius was another favourite source. But there are a number of other factors

which I wish to consider briefly before closing. I mention them
not for their influence on Aquinas but as an indication of the tendency to fuse or confuse Aristotle and Platonism before his time.
We have seen that twelfth century Spain was the most important
source for the transmission of the Aristotelian corpus. The main
reason for this was the great Moslem civilisation, the magnifi-
cence of which still marks cities of the south like Granada, Seville
and Cordoba.[5] Averroes was born in that last city, and Averroes
thought that the mind of Aristotle had reached the limits of
human perfection. He continued the tradition of Aristotelian
studies in the Arab world, which in turn had taken over the work
of the Syrian translators in the expansion of Islamic power. Alkin-
di, Alfarabi and Avicenna (98C-1037) were the greatest of the predecessors of Averroes: they all lived in the East of the Arab world,
but the unity of Isalamic civilisation meant that their work trav-
elled eventually to the West. Avicenna and Averroes were the
best known of these Arab commentators in the time of St Thomas.
Both of them, and particularly Averroes, were concerned with the
presentation of the pure Aristotle, but neither could avoid the
mingling of some elements from Neoplatonism, particularly in relation to God.

One work which helped considerably in the fusion or confusion of Aristotle and Platonism in Moslem thought was the so-
called *Theology* of Aristotle. This work is in fact made up largely of
passages from the last three books of the *Enneads*: the parallels can
be seen in the Henry-Schwyzer edition which prints them on facing pages. Wilson believes that this was vrritten in Syriac by a
monk and translated into Arabic as early as 840. (It was retranslat-
ed into Latin by Aquinas' friend William of Moerbeke.) It must be
emphasised that the great Moslem philosophers were very much
concerned with theology and anxious to provide it with a sound
philosophical framework. The fact that they were philosophers
meant that their orthodoxy was all the more carefully scrutinised.
Neoplatonism would seem to some the very model of a religious
philosophy. So it is not surprising that, as Wallis says, 'the *Theology's* influence was as important as that of Aristotle's own *Metaphysics* and not even Averroes, despite his desire to return from
Avicenna's Neoplatonism to a stricter Arlstotelianism, could
wholly reject its ideas'. (op cit p 164) Aquinas was, of course, not a
man to accept uncritically everything attributed by earlier authorities to Aristotle, but in view of the fusion in the Arabic tradition it
was extremely difficult for him always to draw a clear line of de-
marcation.

Aquinas' critical powers are shown in his attitude to the work known as *Liber de Causis*. This again was taken to be a work of Aristotle's, but was in fact a collection which derived from Proclus' *Elements of Theology*. That it was not simply a work of Aristotle was known to Albert the Great;[6] Thomas came to realise that it was based on the *Elements* (v. his intr. to *In De Causis*) which was translated into Latin by William of Moerbeke.

But the *De Causis* had already been influential in Arabic and Latin. It belonged to the metaphyaics course in the university 1230-1240, and is listed with the works of Aristotle in the Charter of Paris University in 1253. Aquinas treats it with respect in both Summas (v. e.g. *SCG* 1, 26; 3, 61; *ST* 1a, 3, 8; 1a, 5, 1 and 2 and passim) and devoted a special work to it.

Aquinas then has preserved the influence of Platonism as well as Aristotelianism in his system and in doing so has passed it on to later theology. With that our survey must end. The Renaisance was to bring back Platonism to a position of dominance in many fields of European culture. I hope that this survey has shown that in theology at least it had never been forgotten for the first twelve Christian centuries.

Notes and Bibliography

NOTES TO PREFACE

1. The background to the Christian doctrines of the Trinity and Incarnation has been set out by Wolfson in *The Philosophy of the Church Fathers* (ed.3, revised, Harvard University Press, Cambridge, Massachusetts 1970).
2. W. Jaeger, *Aristoteles* (Berlin 1923). English translation by R. Robinson (*Aristotle*, ed. 2, OUP, London 1948). Convenient summaries of the reaction to Jaeger's work are to be found in M. Grene, *A Portrait of Aristotle* (Faber & Faber, London 1963); A.H. Chroust, 'The first thirty years of modern Aristotelian scholarship,' *Classica et Mediaevalia* XXIV (1963) 27-57; I Düring, *Aristoteles* (Carl Winter Universitätsverlag, Heidelberg 1966); G. Lloyd, *Aristotle* (CUP, Cambridge 1968). The *Symposia Aristotelica* are particularly interesting from this point of view.
3. R.T. Wallis, *Neoplatonism* (Duckworth, London 1972), 41.

NOTES TO CHAPTER ONE

1. W. Guthrie, *A History of Greek Philosophy* vol. 1 (CUP, Cambridge 1962), 153. 'The history of Pythagoreanism is perhaps the most controversial subject in all Greek philosophy,' ibid. 146, & v. foll., esp 148 ff for the reasons.
2. The authenticity of the *Alcibiades* and of this particular passage have been questioned, but without good grounds, I think.
3. See W. Theiler, *Zur Geschichte der teleologischen Naturbetrachtung bis auf Aristoteles*, (Zurich 1925).

Bibliography

Texts: Diels Kranz, *Die Fragmente der Vorsokratiker* (ed. 10, 3 vols., Berlin 1960-1); Kirk-Raven, *The Presocratic Philosophers* (CUP, Cambridge 1957). J. Barnes, *Early Greek Philosophy*, (Penguin, London 1987) gives the fragments in translation.
Modern works: Guthrie's *History* (note 1), vols. 1-3, deals with the Presocratics & Socrates and gives a very full bibliography. See also E. Hussey , *The Presocratics* (Duckworth, London 1972), L.P.

Gerson, *God and Greek Philosophy*, (Routledge, London 1990) and, of course, Jaeger's *Theology* mentioned in the preface.

NOTES TO CHAPTER TWO

1. Cf. *Rep.* 500C; *Timaeus* 90A; *Laws* 716B, and see H. Merki, *Homoiosis Theo*, (Freiburg 1952).
2. See my *Plato's Unwritten Teaching*, (Talbot Press, Dublin 1973).
3. For the later history, see J. Whittaker, 'Epekeina Nou Kai Ousias,' *Vigiliae Christianae* 23 (1969) 91-104.
4. *DN* 701D-704A.
5. See R. Dörries' paper in *Entretiens V*, 'Les Sources de Plotin', (Fondation Hardt, Geneva 1960) 194-6.
6. For the debate, see Dillon, John, *The Middle Platonists*, (Duckworth, London 1977) under 'world' in index.

Bibliography

Text: Oxford Classical Texts, ed. Burnet (Clarendon Press, Oxford 1900-7).

English translations: Many excellent modern translations are now available in the Penguin series, and older work with commentary by, e.g. Cornford and Hackforth should not be ignored. A one volume Plato in translation by various hands is Hamilton-Cairns, *Plato*, (Pantheon Books, New York 1961, Princeton University Press, Princeton 1982).

Modern Works: Guthrie's *History.*, vols. 4 and 5, contains full bibliographies on Plato, but as remarked in my preface, and by J.B. Skemp in his review of modern literature, *Plato* (Clarendon Press, Oxford 1976) p 56, there has been little discussion of Plato's theology recently. But see F. Solmsen, *Plato's Theology* (Cornell University Press, Ithaca 1942); Entretiens Tome I, 'La notion du divin depuis Homere jusqu' a Platon' (Fondation Hardt, Vandoeuvres Geneva 1954), especially Verdenius on 'Platons Gottesbegriff'; R. Hackforth, 'Plato's Theism' in *Studies in Plato's Metaphysics*, ed. by R.E. Allen (RKP, London 1965); J.B. Skemp, 'Plato's Concept of Deity' in *Zetesis* (de Strycker Festschrift, Antwerp and Utrecht 1973). E.R. Dodds, 'The Parmenides of Plato and the Origin of the Neoplatonic "One"', *CQ* 22 (1928) is of fundamental importance for the Platonic tradition.

NOTES TO CHAPTER THREE

1. C. Hartshorne in *Royal Institute of Philosophy Lectures*, vol. 2 (London 1967-8), 162.
2. A.H. Chroust, *Aristotle*, vol. 2 (RKP, London 1973), 18.

3. See note 2 to Preface.

4. L. Elders, *Aristotle's Theology* (Van Gorcum, Assen 1972), 10.

5. W. Guthrie, *The Greeks and their Gods* (Methuen, London 1950), 366.

6. Elders, op cit 65. See 50ff for a full discussion of the most recent theories.

7. See again Theiler's work, note 3 to chapter One.

8. W.D. Ross, *Aristotle's Physics* (Clarendon Press, Oxford 1936), 99.

9. Ross, comment on *Met.* 1071 b 8.

10. See W. Maas, *Unveränderlichkeit Gottes* (Schöningh, Munich 1974).

11. J.B. Skemp, *The Theory of Motion in Plato's Later Dialogues* (ed. 2, Amsterdam 1967), xiii.

Bibliography

Text: Ross' edition of the *Metaphysics* (Clarendon Press, Oxford 1924) contains not only the Greek text and a very useful commentary, but also an essay in the introduction on Aristotle's theology. English translation in the Oxford translation, Loeb and Everyman.

Modern works: Elders, op cit above, contains a wide range of references, as do Chroust's two volumes.

NOTES TO CHAPTER FOUR

1. See A.A. Long, *Hellenistic Philosophy*, (Duckworth, London 1974) 15 and 109.

2. F.H. Sandbach, *The Stoics* (Chatto & Windus, London 1975), 72. See all this page on *logos*.

3. Long, op cit, 8.

4. Sandbach, op cit , 70.

Bibliography

Texts: Stoicorum Veterum Fragmenta (SVF), ed by J. von Arnim in 4 vols (Reprinted Teubner, Stuttgart 1968). C.J. de Vogel, *Greek Philosophy* vol. 3 (E. J. Brill, Leiden 1959) is very useful for both Stoics and Epicureans. For the latter, see H. Usener, *Epicurea* (Leipzig 1887); C. Bailey, *Epicurus* (Clarendon Press, Oxford 1926); G. Arrighetti, *Epicura: Opere* (Turin 1960). The Loeb translations of Diogenes Laertius, Sextus Empiricus and Lucretius will all prove useful for English readers.

Modern works: Long and Sandbach provide up-to-date bibliographies. See also J.M. Rist, *Stoic Philosophy* (CUP, Cambridge 1969) and *Epicurus: An Introduction* (CUP, Cambridge 1972).

NOTES TO CHAPTER FIVE

1. John Dillon, *The Middle Platonists* (Duckworth, London 1977), 45.
2. See P. Merlan, *From Platonism to Neoplatonism* (ed. 2, Martinus Nijhoff, The Hague 1960), 96-140.
3. Guthrie, *History.*, vol. 5, 474.
4. Merlan in *Cambridge History of Later Greek and Early Medieval Philosophy*, 35.
5. Dillon, op cit, 2.
6. For a brief, balanced discussion, see J. M. Rist, *Eros and Psyche* (University of Toronto, Toronto 1964), 61 ff, and *De Vogel* III p 401.
7. See H.J. Kramer, *Der Ursprung der Geistmetaphysik* (P. Schippers, Amsterdam 1964), 21ff, esp 42.
8. Merlan in *Cambridge History*, 107 (Note 4 above).
9. See R.T. Wallis, *Neoplatonism* (Duckworth, London 1972), 28.
10. Dillon, op cit, 24.
11. See Chadwick in *Cambridge History*, 143 for references.
12. See the discussion in Dillon, op cit, 313.

Bibliography

Texts: We have only fragments of Speusippus (Lang) and Xenocrates (Heinze). These and more recent studies are drawn on by De Vogel, vol.II. Kramer's *Ursprung* provides a great deal of material for both thinkers, with commentary. *Theophrastus' Metaphysics*, edited with introduction, translation and commentary by W.D. Ross and T.H. Fobes (Oxford 1929, Hildesheim 1967). The Loeb texts and translations are most convenient for Philo and Plutarch. Atticus fragments collected by J. Baudry (Paris 1931). Albinus in vol. 6 of Hermann's edition of *Plato* (Leipzig 1921-36); Budé ed. P. Louis (Paris 1945). Apuleius ed. J. Beaujeu (Paris 1973 Budé). Numenius ed. E. des Places (Paris 1973 Budé).
Modern works: Apart from those mentioned under texts, for Speusippus and Xenocrates see the relevant sections of Dillon, op cit, 12 ff; Guthrie, *History.*, vol.5, 457 ff; and Merlan in *Cambridge History*, 30ff, with the latter also, 107 ff, for Theophrastus. Dillon's survey of Middle Platonism is excellent, and I have drawn on it heavily. The same period is covered by Merlan and Chadwick in the *Cambridge History*. See also, for Philo, É Bréhier, *Les Idées philosophiques et religeuses de Philon d'Alexandrie* (ed. 3, Paris 1950), and, for Albinus, R.E. Witt, *Albinus and the History of Middle Platonism* (Cambridge 1937), together with J.H. Loenen, 'Albinus' Metaphysics: An Attempt at Rehabilitation', *Mnemosyne* Series IV, vols. IX and X. In general, see P. Merlan, *From Platonism to Neoplatonism* (ed. 2, Martinus Nijhoff, The Hague 1960); Entretiens III, 'Re-

cherches sur la tradition platonicienne,' and V, 'Les sources de
Plotin' (Fondation Hardt, Vandoeouvres Geneva 1957 and 1960
respectively); and *Naturphilosophie bei Aristoteles und Theophrast*,
ed. I. Düring (Heidelberg 1969), esp. Skemp's article, which is
very interesting for the problem of the unmoving in Plato, Aristotle and Theophrastus.

NOTES TO CHAPTER SIX

1. For Ammonius, see now particularly the first two contributions, by Dodds and Theiler, to Entretiens Tome V, 'Les Sources
de Plotin'.
2. I emphasise here the writings themselves, because it is as important with him as with Plato to get an impression of the style of
the man. This style has been improved by the rendering into English by MacKenna but the content has not, I think, suffered sub-
stantially. Armstrong's version is more accurate. I use MacKenna's translation throughout this chapter with occasional slight
modifications or additions for the sake of clarity. MacKenna's
translation, edited by John Dillon, is now available in Penguin
(1991).
3. See Bidez, *Vie de Porphyre* , (Leipzig 1913)) 20.
4. E. Lamberz, (Leipzig 1975) in Teubner series.
5. See J. M. Rist, 'Mysticism and Transcendence in Later Neoplatonism', *Hermes* 92 (1964) esp 223 ff on possible modifications of
Plotinianism by Porphyry. Porphyry's waverings must always be
kept in mind: see Hadot in Entretiens XII, 'Porphyre' (Fondation
Hardt, Vandoeuvres Geneva 1966), 131f, and the Budé editors of
De Abstinentia, XLIII on the 'stupéfiant' contradiction in II 46.

Bibliography

Plotinus:
Text: *Enneads*, ed. P. Henry and H.R. Schwyzer (Oxford Classical
Texts, Clarendon Press, Oxford 1964-1983, 3 vols). A.H. Armstrong (Loeb Classical Library, Harvard University Press, London
and Cambridge, Mass. 1966-88). English translations by Armstrong, and by Stephen MacKenna (ed. 4, revised, Dillon, 1991, Faber & Faber, London 1969).
Modern works: Entretiens Tome V, 'Les Sources de Plotin' (Fondation Hardt, Vandoeuvres, Geneva 1960); W. Theiler, *Die Vorberei-
tung des Neuplatonismus* (Weidmann, Berlin 1930,1964); A.H. Armstrong, *Cambridge History of Later Greek and Early Medieval
Philoscphy* (CUP, Cambridge 1967), 195-268; J. M. Rist, *Plotinus: the*

Road to Reality (CUP, Cambridge 1967); R.T. Wallis, *Neoplatonism* (Duckworth, London 1972).

Porphyry:

Texts: Letter to Anebo, ed. A.R. Sodano (Naples 1958); *Sententiae*, ed. E. Lamberz (Leipzig 1975); *Ad Marcellam*, ed. W. Potscher (E. J. Brill, Leiden 1969); *De l'abstinence*, ed. Bouffartigue/Patillon (Belles Lettres, Paris 1977); *De Regressu Animae*, in Bidez, *Vie de Porphyre*; *Miscellaneous Enquiries*, ed. H. Dörrie (Munich 1959); *Against the Christians*, ed. A. Harnack (Berlin 1916). Cf. also Parmenides commentary, ed. P. Hadot in *Porphyre et Victorinus* (Paris 1968); *Oracles Chaldaiques*, ed. E. des Places (Belles Lettres, Paris 1971).

Modern works: Entretiens Tome XII, 'Porphyre' (Fondation Hardt, Vandoeuvres Geneva 1966); R.T. Wallis, op cit ; A.C. Lloyd, in *CHLGEMP*, 272-325.

Iamblichus:

Texts: De Mysteriis, ed. E. des Places (Paris 1966); *On the Soul*: see A.J. Festugière, *La Révélation d'Hermès Trismégiste*, vol. iii; Fragmenta, ed. J. Dillon (E. J. Brill, Leiden 1973). For others see bibliography in *CHLGEMP*.

Modern Works: Entretiens Tome XXI, 'De Iamblique a Proclus' (Fondation Hardt, Vandoeuvres Geneva 1975); Wallis, op cit; Lloyd, in op cit.

Proclus:

Texts: Elements of Theology, ed. E.R. Dodds (ed. 2, Clarendon Press, Oxford 1963); *Platonic Theology*, ed. H. D. Saffrey and L. G. Westerink (Belles Lettres, Paris 1968); *Tria Opuscula*, ed. H. Boese (Berlin 1970). See also Wallis and *CHLGEMP* bibliographies.

Modern works: as under Iamblichus.

NOTES TO CHAPTER SEVEN

1. R.A. Markus, *CHLGEMP*, 332.

2. See *Traités theologiques sur la Trinite*, ed. P. Henry and P. Hadot (Sources Chrétiennes, Du Cerf, Paris 1960), 7ff for chronology, writings etc.

3. See also A A. III i, 40 on God as 'cessans vita'; 2, 31 ff; IV 8, 26 ff; 16,29 ff.

4. See AA I 49, 26 ff with Hadot's note on Celsus and Nicholas of Cusa.

5. See P. Courcelle, *Recherches sur les 'Confessions' de S. Augustin* (Editions E. de Boccard, Paris 1950), 99ff, and P. Brown's note on the reaction, *Augustine of Hippo* (Faber & Faber, London 1967),86.

6. See Theiler, *Porphyrios und Augustin* (Halle 1933), 238; Brown,

op cit, 96.

7. See Courcelle, op cit, 100.

8. D. Knowles, *The Evolution of Medieval Thought* (Longmans, London 1962), 53.

9. P. Courcelle, *La Consolation de Philosophie dans la tradition Litteraire* (Études augustiniennes, Paris 1967), 171.

Bibliography

Texts: For Candidus and Victorinus, see note 2 above. For Augustine's *Confessions*, see Solignac in *Bibliotheque Augustinienne*, sér, ii, 13-14, 1962. Frank Sheed's English translation (Sheed & Ward, London 1944) is recommended, but the Penguin translation is probably more accessible. Henry Chadwick (OUP, Oxford 1991) is excellent. For other works of St Augustine, see the chronological tables in Brown's *Augustine of Hippo* which also contain lists of English translations available. For Boethius I have used the Loeb text and translation, modifying when necessary.

Modern works: All three writers are treated in parts V and VII of the *Cambridge History* q.v. The bibliography on Augustine is enormous, but there are good guides in the *Cambridge History* and Brown. Courcelle's work and Brown's are basic. For Boethius, see also E.K. Rand, *Founders of the Middle Ages* (Harvard University Press, Cambridge, Mass. 1928). Courcelle's work (note 9) is again basic.

NOTES TO CHAPTER EIGHT

1. J.P. Sheldon-Williams, *Johannis Scotti Eriugenae Periphyseon* Book I (Dublin Institute for Advanced Studies, Dublin 1968), VII.

2. E. Gilson, *History of Christian Philosophy in the Middle Ages* (Sheed & Ward, London 1955), 81.

3. For an excellent discussion, see *Denys L'Aréopagite La Hiérarchie Céleste*, introduction by R. Roques (Sources Chretiennes, Du Cerf, Paris 1958), viiff.

4. See J.J. O'Meara, *Eriugena* (Mercier Press, Cork 1969), 20.

5. See O'Meara, op cit,14 ff; M. Cappuyns, *Jean Scot Érigène* (Abbaye du Mont César, Louvain 1933), 128 ff; and Sheldon-Williams in *CHLGEMP*, 519.

6. There is a good brief description of the origins of this in *CHLG.*, 521ff.

7. 'Qui melius nesciendo scitur,' repeated in 687A and see 771C: a motif from St Augustine.

8. See *CHLG.*, 523.

9. Parma ed. 1964, 346.

10. Roques' introduction (note 3 above), XI is again excellent on this.

11. Cappuyns op cit, 251, 245ff.

12. *CHLG.*, 533.

Bibliography

Work is still progressing on Eriugena and on Pseudo-Dionysius, but we are still too dependent on Migne's Patrology in Latin and Greek. Mary Brennan has published a very full bibliography of Eriugena in *Studi Medievali XVIII* (1977), 401-447. Roques (note 3) and Sheldon-Williams in the *Cambridge History* provide bibliographies for Pseudo-Dionysius. Sheldon-Williams has translated the first two books of the *Periphyseon*, and C. E. Rolt *The Divine Names* and *The Mystical Theology* in *Dionysius the Areopagite* (New edition, SPCK, London 1940). This divides according to the chapters and sections of Migne and I have cited these as well as the Migne columns as seemed suitable.

NOTES TO CHAPTER NINE

1. Knowles, op cit, 188ff.

2. Gilson, *Christian Philosophy*, 278 and notes.

3. A. Kenny, *The Five Ways* (RKP, London 1969), 71.

4. Kenny, ibid, 77ff.

5. Copleston, *History of Philosophy*, vol. 2. 186ff; Knowles, op cit, 193ff; Gilson, op cit, 177ff.

6. Gilson, op cit, 637.

Bibliography

Summa Theologiae (London 1963 75) has the Latin text and English translation. *Summa Contra Gentiles* (ed. 2, Paris 1881) is available in English as *On the Truth of the Catholic Faith* (Random House, 1955). Compact and useful accounts of Aquinas' thought are Copleston's *Aquinas* (Penguin, Harmondsworth, Middlesex, 1955) and A. Kenny's *Aquinas* (Past Masters, OUP, Oxford 1980).